REAL FOOD, REALLY FAST

REAL FOOD, REALLY FAST

Delicious **Plant-Based** Recipes Ready in 10 Minutes or Less

HANNAH KAMINSKY

Skyhorse Publishing

Skyhorse Publishing books may be purchased in bulk at special discounts for sales promotion, corporate gifts, fund-raising, or educational purposes. Special editions can also be created to specifications. For details, contact the Special Sales Department, Skyhorse Publishing, 307 West 36th Street, 11th Floor, New York, NY 10018 or info@skyhorsepublishing.com.

Skyhorse® and Skyhorse Publishing® are registered trademarks of Skyhorse Publishing, Inc.®, a Delaware corporation.

Visit our website at www.skyhorsepublishing.com.

10 9 8 7 6 5 4 3 2 1

Library of Congress Cataloging-in-Publication Data is available on file.

Cover design by Jane Sheppard

Cover photo credit: Hannah Kaminsky

Print ISBN: 978-1-5107-2759-5
Ebook ISBN: 978-1-5107-2760-1

Printed in China

Contents

Introduction

"Quick and easy" recipes are a dime a dozen, or perhaps a penny a dozen is more accurate at the current exchange rate, and yet our recipe files still come up empty when dinnertime rolls around. Delve into those stacks of dusty cookbooks and troll the Internet for something simple and you'll be rewarded with an avalanche of options. Why seek out even more? Quite simply, it's rare that these recipes live up to their lofty promises. Flavor and nutrition suffer in the name of speed, yielding to the temptations of modern convenience foods that pale in comparison to something a bit fresher. Go the more wholesome route, and suddenly you're tacking on an extra 20 minutes of prep time that the recipe author conveniently failed to mention. Adding insult to injury, for every hundred formulas floating about in various formats, only one might have any culinary merit—and that's being generous. What could be worse than going through the work of cooking from scratch after an already exhausting day of work only to sit down to a flavorless meal?

End the madness here and now. These recipes are guaranteed to pull no punches, won't leave a bad taste in your mouth, or force you to walk away hungry. Fussy foods have no place on my plate;

I'd rather pour myself a bowl of cereal at night than go through any greater hassle to feed myself, so I'd never ask more of anyone I care about. Every option, from breakfast to dessert, has been put through the gantlet, torture tested to make sure the recipe can hold up to tight deadlines and even shorter tempers. Ten minutes or less is the magic number. With a few of the tips and tricks scattered throughout the book, you can handily whip up a feast in less time than it takes to put in a delivery order online.

Though this seemingly crazy, self-imposed time limit may be the inspiration, it's far from the most important guiding factor to the collection of plant-based treats that await you. Flavor always comes first. If it doesn't make your kitchen smell irresistible and your palate sing, it doesn't make the cut, no questions asked. After all, food should do more than just fill your stomach! Cut the crappy ingredients, dump the same old standbys, and start dancing to a new culinary rhythm, no matter how busy the daily grind gets. This is not just another "quick and easy" vegan cookbook.

Warp-Speed Secrets and Fast Fundamentals

The single most important ingredient in any recipe can't be measured in tablespoons or cups, nor can it be bought, borrowed, or stolen. That extra piece of the puzzle that most cookbooks fail to address is *you*, the intrepid cook, boldly venturing forth to explore new culinary territory. Anyone can read a recipe and it doesn't take a classically trained chef to chop an onion, but there are certain steps that can be taken to speed through prep work in record time. To accomplish the following formulas in under 10 minutes as promised, before you prepare your vegetables, you must prepare yourself. Move with intention and a sense of urgency; know your next step before you get there to keep dancing through the routine with grace. That also means reading through each recipe from start to finish so there are no surprises halfway through the hustle.

Whether you're a seasoned pro or a new cook, the following suggestions should help tune up your techniques to get food on the table faster than ever before. Keep your eyes peeled for additional "quick tips" sprinkled throughout the book to help speed up specific recipes, too!

Maximize Your Microwave

Lacking the ability to properly brown foods, microwaves are frequently discredited as "real" cooking equipment, but they're incredibly handy for powering specific techniques. Quickly thaw out frozen vegetables before tossing them into a soup or stew, effectively cooking them before they ever hit the stove, simultaneously raising their temperature to prevent the heat from dropping when they dive in. No matter what, always drain thoroughly before using. Depending on how long the frozen goods have been in the chill chest, additional moisture from within the freezer may have built up on the surface, and the last thing you want is for that excess to water down your dinner.

Microwaves are good for so much more than simply defrosting, though. They're my preferred appliance when it comes to toasting nuts, seeds, and coconut in the blink of an eye. Spread out the ingredients in an even layer on a large plate, leaving the center clear (since it tends to cook less evenly.) Heat for 1–3 minutes, depending on the particular ingredient and quantity, stirring every 30 seconds or so to ensure an even, golden roast. It tends to move very quickly from raw to burnt, so you must keep a close eye on the process from start to finish.

Take Stock

The best recipe is one that you don't need to shop for, and by stocking up on a few essential staples, you may be impressed at what you can accomplish without an extra trip to the store. Canned and dry goods that have a virtually endless shelf life are always smart buys, prime candidates for purchasing in bulk whenever possible. For anyone beginning to build their own cooking pantry, these are the bare basics that I personally keep on hand at all times:

Quick Cooking Grains and Starches:

Couscous
Small Pasta Shapes
Tortillas, Bread, or Pita
All-Purpose Flour
Cornstarch

Nuts & Seeds:

Whole Flaxseed
Almonds
Cashews
Chia Seeds

Canned / Packaged:

Beans
Tomato Paste
Nutritional Yeast
Crushed and/or Diced Tomatoes
Marinara Sauce
Soy Sauce
Apple Cider Vinegar
Vegetable Stock Powder
Olive Oil
Coconut Oil
Various Spices and Dried Herbs

Chop to It

While anyone can pick up a knife and immediately accomplish some serious plant-based butchery, it's equally as important to hone your knife skills as it is to keep your blade sharp. If you're not quite confident breaking down basic vegetables, hit up YouTube and find an endless trove of helpful visual assistance. More crucial than the actual cut, however, is consistency. Keep all pieces of uniform size to ensure proper, even cooking. As they say, practice makes perfect; cook more often and you'll cook better overall!

Frozen Assets

The more you can prepare in advance, the faster you can throw together a full meal later. On weekends or quiet days, I like to do a big grocery shop and break down as many of the vegetables as possible, tossing them into the freezer for future recipes. That means chopping onions, mincing or roasting garlic, roasting peppers, peeling and slicing ripe bananas, and dicing or shredding potatoes, tossing them into individual ziplock bags, and stashing them in the freezer until hunger strikes. Label each bag clearly with the contents, quantity, and date so you'll know what you're looking at later.

The same can be done with fresh herbs to add instant pops of vibrant flavor. Remove any tough stems and place the leaves into your blender or food processor, along with a splash of water—just enough to keep things moving and break down the herbs. Pulse until very finely minced, pausing to scrape down the sides of the container as needed. Transfer tablespoons or teaspoons of the coarse paste to ice cube trays (ideally made of silicone for easiest removal) and let chill out in the freezer until solidified. This will give you distinct measures that are much easier to use than one giant chunk, so try to seek out smaller shapes that will be more accommodating for more scant measurements. Bag and tag the cubes as with the vegetables for final storage. Simply pop a cube into the finished dish at the very last moment, allowing the residual heat to thaw the herbs, to maintain their flavor integrity.

Embroiled in Oven Usage

It generally takes too long to fully preheat an oven if you want to squeeze in dinner with 10 minutes or less to spare, but that doesn't mean the appliance is obsolete. The broiler turns on at full blast the instant it's activated, so you can brown or crisp anything in less time than it will take to set the table. Make the most of this ingenious feature to quickly toast a whole loaf of bread or effortlessly sear proteins. Just bear in mind that this intense heat can only penetrate the very top of the food and thus can't cook thicker pieces all the way through. Anything that's intended to be served warm must already be hot when it goes under the flame. Additionally, saucy or soupy foods should be set over a baking pan or dish to capture any bubbly drips, preventing them from falling to the bottom of the oven and burning. See page 8 for more broiler basics.

The Spice Is Right

Spice is the variety of life, or so the saying goes. Spices are the foundation of flavor, an irreplaceable component in every recipe. That said, the sheer range of distinct seasonings can be overwhelming to consider, especially with limited time, storage space, or discretionary spending. When you can't invest in a fully furnished spice rack, there's no shame in springing for a few select blends. Draft your own spicy team based on your taste preferences, but I've personally gotten the most mileage out of mixes for madras curry powder, Italian seasoning, Creole seasoning, and chili powder.

Can You Hack It?

Why cut and chop with conventional techniques when you can hack your way to faster food prep? Some specific foods hold secret shortcuts that will leave traditional methods in the dust.

- *Citrus:* Always zest lemons, oranges, and limes first, before slicing or juicing. While they're still whole you'll have more surface area to work with, and a better base to hold so you're less likely to grate your fingers at the same time. Then, to extract the most juice possible, microwave for 10–15 seconds to gently warm, and roll them firmly against the counter to break down some of the cell walls before cutting in half and squeezing.

- *Garlic:* Separate the cloves and give each one a sharp whack with the side of your knife to instantly loosen the skins. You should be able to pick the peel right off. Once cleaned, you can continue smashing and mashing them with the side of the knife, rather than the blade, to yield a quick, coarse paste that can be used instead of a fine mince.

- **Ginger:** Don't bother breaking out the peeler to remove the tough outer skin. Use a paring knife to shave away the exterior if needed, but better yet, buy very young, fresh ginger that doesn't need to be peeled in the first place. In Japanese markets, this is referred to as "myoga."

- **Cauliflower or Broccoli:** Pare away the leaves and trim down the excess stem. Place the head in a large, clean plastic bag, and twist it closed. Bang the whole thing down on the counter repeatedly, stem-side first, to easily break it down into bite-sized florets.

- **Cherry Tomatoes:** Instead of chasing around each tasty red marble and slicing them in half one by one, slash straight through a whole batch in one fell swoop. Place a generous handful between two plates and gently press down to keep them all stable and still. Use an exceptionally sharp knife to cut horizontally through the center to cleanly halve tomatoes.

- **Corn:** Once cooked, shuck corn quickly by slicing off the bottom of the husk and simply pushing the ear out, leaving the messy silk behind.

- **Cherries:** Don't bother with a uni-tasking cherry pitter if you're unlikely to use it more than once or twice a year. Place each cherry on top of an empty glass soda or beer bottle, and use a chopstick to poke out the pit, pushing it straight down into the bottle.

- **Nondairy Milk:** Whip up an instant dairy-free beverage by simply combining 2 tablespoons of your favorite nut butter (almond and cashew are my favorite options, but sunflower, peanut, and pecan are also excellent alternatives) with 1 cup of water in your blender. Blend until smooth and use as is for savory cooking or baking, or add up to a tablespoon of sugar, agave, or maple syrup to sweeten it for drinking.

Essential Equipment

Quick cooking means employing as few fancy kitchen tools and toys as possible, both for speeding through the preliminary preparation, and reducing the number of dirty dishes to attend to afterwards. Gadget enthusiasts are welcome to add more specialized equipment into the fray, but at bare minimum, you'll need a few large bowls, saucepans, a working stove, and a heaping helping of enthusiasm. While all the rest is non-obligatory, a few technological shortcuts will certainly make the work move along more easily. The following suggestions are a few options that may aid in your culinary adventures.

Blender

They come in all shapes and sizes, with wildly varying prices to match. If you want the sturdiest machine that will grant you the most pureeing power, I can't recommend the Vitamix highly enough. Yes, it's one of the priciest models on the market for consumer purchase, but it actually is professional quality and will pay for itself through saved time and aggravation. There is simply nothing else that can blend whole nuts so silky smooth, or grind whole beans down to perfectly fine flour. I use mine almost every day, whether for baking adventures or just blending myself a smoothie.

Broiler

If you've never used it before, you're missing out on one of the best elements built right into your oven. It reaches scorching-hot temperatures in seconds, providing instant fire power when you want to quickly brown surfaces or finish a dish with a touch of char. You can also use the broiler in toaster ovens for greater efficiency, since less heat is lost in smaller, more confined space. Set the rack as close to the heating element as possible to maximize that intensity and exposure. Unlike baking, broiling is most effective when the door to the oven is left slightly ajar to prevent steam from building up, preventing a proper dry sear.

Food Processor

They both have a spinning blade at the bottom of a sealed canister, but don't consider a blender and a food processor as being interchangeable in every procedure. There's no way you'd be able to make pastry dough in a blender, but my food processor is the secret to effortlessly whipping up everything from silky-smooth hummus to flaky crust. If you have a limited budget for only one serious appliance investment, go for a food processor. Choose a model with at least 7–8 cups capacity, or else be prepared to process many recipes in batches.

Kitchen Torch

Hasn't every child wanted their own flamethrower growing up? Okay, maybe I was just an odd child, but there's no denying the allure of playing with fire. A kitchen torch allows you that thrill with a bit more safety. Found in kitchen supply and specialty shops, these devices look somewhat like small guns and are powered by butane. Very reasonably priced at $10–$20 for most basic models, they make brûléeing or browning meringue a breeze.

Mandoline

No relation to the mandolin, a stringed musical instrument that resembles a banjo, the mandoline is the secret to deconstructing produce into perfect paper-thin slices, all the exact same width, without needing to pick up a knife. The frame can be made of plastic or metal and comes with numerous inserts that will adjust the width of the finished slices. Some even come with specialty attachments that will create waffle cuts and crinkle cuts, ideal for fancy French fries. A common misconception is that they're dangerous, but this only rings true when used improperly, like any other tool. Never, ever, EVER operate a mandoline without the hand guard. I know far too many people, including myself, that have nearly lost fingers trying to beat the system and go it alone. That one last tiny slice off the bottom of that slippery potato just isn't worth the pain.

Microwave

Did you know that the first microwave ever built was 6 feet tall, weighed 750 pounds, and cost $5,000? Vast technological advances have brought down all of those figures significantly, allowing the machines to become ubiquitous kitchen staples today. Few people give their microwaves a second thought, but different models can vary greatly in power and capacity. The average electromagnetic oven has an output of 700 watts, which is what most recipes are written to accommodate. If you're not sure about your own microwave, place a cup of water in a dish and see how long it takes to boil. For a 700 watt model, it should take about 2½ minutes; 1000 watts will get you there in only 1¾ minutes. Rarely will you encounter a non-commercial machine that pumps out over 1200 watts, which will boil water in under 1½ minutes. Once you harness the full power of your machine, adjust your cooking times accordingly. You can also find a more thorough conversion chart at MicrowaveWatt.com.

Piping / Pastry Bags and Tips

The very first time I picked up a piping bag to frost a cupcake, I knew that there was no going back. It just makes for a more professional presentation than frosting blobbed on with a knife. Piping bags are by no means necessary tools, but rather a baker's luxury. If you don't know how to wield a pastry bag or cannot be bothered with the hassle, there is no need to run out and buy one. However, should you wish to give piping a try, don't skimp on the quality! Piping bags come in heavy-duty, reusable fabric or plastic and disposable varieties, which range in quality. This is one time when I like to use disposable, because piping bags really are a nightmare to clean. Just avoid the cheaper plastic bags, as they are often too thin to stand up to the pressure. As for the tips, you only need one or two big star tips to make a nice "swirly" design. You can also pipe straight out of the bag for a rounded spiral.

Silpats®

I simply adore these flat, nonstick mats and use them at every opportunity. Likened to reusable parchment paper, Silpats cut down on the cost and excess waste of traditional single-use fibers. In terms of performance, Silpats also tend to reduce browning, so that it is more difficult (but by no means impossible) to burn cookies when using them. While one should last you several years, it is helpful to have a few on hand. For best care, wash them promptly after each use with mild soap and a soft sponge. Silpats can be located at any decent kitchen store and many grocery stores in the housewares aisle.

Spiralizer

Once an esoteric uni-tasking tool used exclusively in raw cuisine, spiralizers have taken the whole world by storm, spinning out curly strands of vegetables with the flick of the wrist. Operated much like a hand-crank pencil sharpener, firm fruits and vegetables can be spun through a series of small blades to make "noodles" or ribbons of various sizes. Zucchini are typically the gateway drug for more daring plant-based pasta facsimiles; I've had wonderful results with seedless cucumbers, carrots, beets, strips of pumpkin, daikon, and parsnips, to name a few. You can find spiralizers sold for $15–$40, and you really don't need to splurge on this small investment, since they're really more or less just as effective. If you're still not quite ready to commit, you can get a similar sort of result from a julienne peeler, but it will take a bit more time and labor to turn out the same volume of skinny strands.

Stand Mixer

While hand mixers get the job done, a good stand mixer will save your arm a tremendous amount of grief. A high-quality stand mixer can be a steep initial investment, but it is usually worth its weight in gold. Powerful and independent, it is easy to multitask while this machine mixes away. If your kitchen space or budget doesn't allow for this luxury, then a hand mixer, or even the vigorous use of a whisk, will work whenever a stand mixer is noted.

Strainer

When I call for one of these in a recipe, chances are I'm not talking about a pasta colander, with its large, spread-out holes. To sieve out raspberry seeds, drain vegan yogurt, or take care of any other liquid/solid separation jobs, a decent fine mesh sieve will tackle the job with ease. Seek out strainers with solid construction, so that the mesh won't pull out after repeated pressings with a spatula. One about 7–9 inches in diameter should accommodate.

Ingredient Glossary

Agave Nectar

Derived from the same plant as tequila but far less potent, this syrup is made from the condensed juice found at the core of the agave cactus. It is available in both light and dark varieties; the dark possesses a more nuanced, complex, and somewhat floral flavor, while the light tends to provide only a clean sweetness. Considered a less refined form of sugar, agave nectar has a much lower glycemic index than many traditional granulated sweeteners, and is therefore consumed by some diabetics in moderation.

All-Purpose Flour

While wonderful flours can be made from all sorts of grains, beans, nuts, and seeds, the gold standard in everyday baking and cooking is still traditional "all-purpose" wheat flour. Falling texturally somewhere in between cake flour and bread flour, it works as a seamless binder, strong foundation, and neutral base. It's an essential pantry staple for me, stocked in my cupboard at all times. All-purpose flour may be labeled in stores as unbleached white flour or simply "plain flour." Gluten-free all-purpose flour is also widely available now in mainstream markets and can be substituted at a 1:1 ratio for those sensitive to wheat. Many different blends exist, but I've personally had good results with Bob's Red Mill®, Cup 4 Cup®, and King Arthur®.

Almond Meal/Flour

Almond flour is nothing more than raw almonds ground down into a fine powder, light and even in consistency which makes it ideal for baking, while almond meal is generally a bit coarser. To make your own, just throw a pound or so of completely unadulterated almonds into your food processor, and pulse until floury. It's helpful to freeze the almonds in advance so that they don't overheat and turn into almond butter. You can also create a finer texture by passing the initial almond meal through a fine sieve to sift out the larger pieces. Due to their high oil content, ground nuts can go rancid fairly quickly. If you opt to stock up and save some for later, be sure to store the freshly ground almond flour in an airtight container in the refrigerator or freezer. To cut down on labor and save a little time, almond flour or meal can be purchased in bulk from natural food stores.

Aquafaba

It's the not-so-secret ingredient taking the world by storm, dubbed a "miracle" by some and a food science breakthrough by others. In case you're not already a fervent fan, aquafaba is the excess liquid found in any ordinary can of chickpeas. Technically, any bean can produce aquafaba, but the unique ratio of protein and starch found in garbanzo beans has been found to best mimic the binding and whipping properties previously only seen in egg whites. Different brands will yield slightly different results, but I've never found any that are complete duds. For more delicate applications like meringues or marshmallow fluff, you can always concentrate your aquafaba to create a stronger foam matrix by cooking it gently over the stove and reducing some of the water.

Arrowroot Powder/Flour

Thanks to arrowroot, you can thicken sauces, puddings, and mousses with ease. This white powder is very similar to kudzu and is often compared to other starchy flours. However, arrowroot is so fine that it produces much smoother, creamier results, and is less likely to stick together and form large lumps. It also thickens liquids much more quickly than cornstarch or potato starch, without leaving an unpleasant, raw sort of cereal flavor behind.

Black Salt (Kala Namak)

Lovingly if crudely nicknamed "fart salt" around these parts, the sulfurous odor released by a big bagful really does smell like . . . well, you can probably guess. Despite that unpromising introduction, it does taste far better, and eerily similar to eggs. Enhancing everything from tofu scrambles to loaves of challah, it's one of those secret ingredients that every vegan should have in their arsenal. Don't let the name confuse you though; the fine grains are actually mottled pink in appearance, not black.

Bragg Liquid Aminos

Made from soybeans and closely resembling traditional soy sauce in both flavor and color, the two can be swapped at a 1:1 ratio if you should ever find your pantry lacking for either. There are very subtle nuances differentiating the taste of the two, making the liquid aminos slightly sweeter and savory in a way that I believe mimics fish sauce more closely. For those with soy sensitivities there are also coconut-based liquid aminos that can be purchased at health food stores or high-end specialty grocers.

Butter

It's a basic kitchen staple, but good dairy-free butter can be quite elusive if you don't know what to look for. Some name brands contain whey or other milk derivatives, while others conceal the elusive, animal-derived vitamin D3, so be alert when scanning ingredient labels. For ease, I prefer to use it in stick form, such as Earth Balance® Buttery Sticks or Miyoko's Kitchen European Style Cultured VeganButter. Never try to substitute spreadable butter from a tub! These varieties have much more water to allow them to spread while cold, and will thus bake and cook differently. I always use unsalted butter unless otherwise noted, but you are welcome to use salted as long as you remove about ¼ teaspoon of salt per ¼ cup of butter from the recipe. Overly salted food is one of the first flaws that diners notice, so take care with your seasoning and always adjust to taste.

Cacao Nibs

Also known as raw chocolate, cacao nibs are unprocessed cacao nuts, simply broken up into smaller pieces. Considerably more earthy and harsh than the sweet, mellow chocolate found in bars or chips, it is often used for texture and accent flavor in desserts. Sometimes it can be found coated in sugar to soften its inherent bitter edge, but for baking or cooking, you'll want to start with the plain, raw version for the most versatility. Seek out bags of cacao nibs in health food stores; if you're really lucky, you may be able to find them in the bulk bins of well-stocked specialty stores.

Carob

Carob gets a bad rap from people who are expecting chocolate but are served this roasted Arabian bean instead. Allowed to shine as not a substitute, but as the best version of itself possible, carob can in fact be quite delicious. Besides, it has the added bonus of being safe to share with our canine friends. Seek out roasted carob powder for the richest flavor.

Chia Seeds

Yes, this is the same stuff that makes chia pets so green and fuzzy, and yes, the seeds are edible! Tiny but mighty, what makes these particular seeds so special is that they form a gel when mixed with liquid. This makes them a powerful binder when trying to replace eggs, or should flaxseeds be in short supply. Store in the freezer for a longer lifespan, and grind them before using in baked goods to maintain an even crumb texture.

Chocolate

Chocolate is chocolate, right? Oh, if only it were so simple. Needless to say, conventional white and milk chocolate are out of the picture, but some so-called dark chocolates still don't make the dairy-free cut. Even those that claim to be "70% cacao solids, extra-special dark" may have milk solids or butterfat lurking within. Don't buy the hype or the fillers! Stay vigilant and check labels for milk-based ingredients, as unadulterated chocolate is far superior. Semisweet has approximately half as much sugar as cocoa solids, and bittersweet tends to have even less. Baker's chocolate is always vegan and entirely unsweetened, so it has intense chocolate flavor, but isn't the tastiest option for eating out of hand. Dark chocolate is somewhat of a catchall term that has no official nor legal definition.

Coconut Milk

When called for in this book, I'm referring to regular, full-fat coconut milk. That fat is necessary for creating a smooth, creamy mouth feel, and of course a richer taste. Light coconut milk or coconut milk beverages found in aseptic containers *may* be suitable in some cases for particularly calorie-conscious cooks, but such a substitution is likely to have detrimental effects on the overall texture of the dish. For best results, treat yourself to the genuine article. Plain coconut milk is found canned in the ethnic foods aisle of the grocery store. You can make it yourself from fresh coconut meat, but in most cases, the added hassle honestly isn't worth the expense or effort.

Coconut Oil

Once demonized as artery-clogging sludge not fit to grease a doorframe, nutritionists now can't recommend this tropical fat highly enough. Touted for its benefits when consumed or used on the skin or hair, it's readily available just about anywhere you turn. Two varieties populate store shelves: Virgin (also labeled as raw or unrefined) coconut oil and refined coconut oil. Virgin gets the best press from the health experts since it's less processed, and it bears the subtle aroma of the coconut flesh. Refined is wonderful for baked goods, however, since it has been deodorized and is essentially flavorless, allowing it to blend seamlessly into any dish. They both solidify below 76°F, but virgin oil reaches its smoke point at 350°F while refined is at 450°F, meaning you can safely use it to fry or roast food at much higher temperatures. Either works fine for raw or unbaked applications, so feel free to choose either one based on how much you want to taste the coconut essence in the final product.

Cocoa Butter

Chocolate is comprised of two key elements: the cocoa solids, which give it that distinct cocoa flavor, and the cocoa butter, which is the fat that provides the body. Cocoa butter is solid at room temperature, like all tropical oils, so it's best to measure it after melting, as the firm chunks can appear deceptively voluminous. It's important to pick up high quality, food grade cocoa butter. As a popular ingredient in body lotions and lip balms, some offerings come with fillers and undesirable additives, so shop carefully if you search locally. Avoid deodorized cocoa butter, unless you'd rather omit its natural flavor from your desserts.

Confectioner's Sugar

Otherwise known as powdered sugar, icing sugar, or 10x sugar, confectioner's sugar is a very finely ground version of standard white sugar, often with a touch of starch included to prevent clumping. You can make your own confectioner's sugar by powdering 1 cup of granulated sugar with 1 tablespoon of cornstarch in your food processor or spice grinder. Simply blend the sugar and cornstarch on the highest speed for about two minutes, allowing the dust to settle before opening your machine—unless you want to inhale a cloud of sugar!

Cream Cheese

Many innovative companies now make dairy-free products that will give you the most authentic shmears and cream cheese frostings imaginable. These soft spreads also hold up beautifully in cookie dough and piecrusts, contributing a great tangy flavor and excellent structure. My favorite brand is the classic Tofutti®, but there are now numerous options available that all work just as well in dessert applications. This ingredient is hard to replace with homemade varieties when seeking smooth, consistent results, so I suggest that you check out your local mega mart or natural food grocer, or head online if all else fails.

Cream of Tartar

Don't let the name fool you; cream of tartar has absolutely nothing to do with either cream or tartar sauce. It is actually created through the fermentation process that grapes undergo in the production of wine. Thus, it can contribute a good deal of acid to recipes in very small doses. Sometimes used as a stabilizer, it can create flavors similar to buttermilk, or be used to create baking powder. For a small batch, sift together 2 tablespoons cream of tartar with 1 tablespoon baking soda and 1 teaspoon cornstarch.

Dehydrated Onion Flakes

Want to know the secret to what makes everything bagels so great? Dehydrated onion flakes. Yes, it's a careful balance of many delightful seeds and seasonings, but the dried onions are what really carry the whole flavor. You might be forgiven for cutting back on any other single component, whereas an allium deficit would throw the entire balance into unrecognizable disarray. Most supermarkets and specialty spice shops such as Penzeys or MySpiceSage.com can accommodate, with the option of toasted onion flakes as well, lending a warmer, roasted note to the blend. You can make your own if you have a dehydrator, or a slow oven and a lot of patience. Just dice two or three onions and spread them out on a nonstick tray or Silpat. Dehydrate for 4–10 hours, or bake in the oven at the lowest setting possible (usually around 160–170°F) for 3–8 hours, stirring periodically, until crisp and papery.

Five-Spice Powder

A powerful mixture of anise, pepper, cinnamon, fennel seed, and cloves, we owe Chinese cuisine for this spicy representation of the five basic tastes—salty, sweet, sour, bitter, and savory. Ratios and exact blends vary depending on who you ask, and every cook seems to have their own family recipe, so go ahead and tweak until it pleases your own palate. Most grocery stores will stock the seasoning in the spice aisle, but here's how I like to mix mine up at home:

2 Tablespoons Ground Star Anise
2 Tablespoons Crushed Cinnamon Stick Pieces
2 Teaspoons Ground Fennel Seeds
2 Teaspoons Crushed Szechuan Peppercorns
¼ Teaspoon Ground Cloves

Toss all the spices into a coffee or spice grinder, and let the machine pulverize everything to a fine powder. Make sure that there are no large pieces or unmixed pockets of spice before transferring to an airtight jar. Dark-colored glass is the best option, because light will degrade the flavors faster.

If you can't find Szechuan peppercorns, an equal amount of either black or white peppercorns can be substituted for a slightly different but similarly fiery bite.

Flavor Extracts

I usually try to stay as far away from flavor extracts as possible, because they are all too often artificial, insipid, and a poor replacement for the real thing. However, vanilla (see page 24 for further details), peppermint, and almond are my main exceptions, as high quality extracts from the actual sources are readily available in most markets. Just make sure to avoid any bottles that list sugar, corn syrup, colors, or chemical stabilizers in addition to your flavor of choice. For more unconventional essences, if your supermarket searches end up unsuccessful, try the Internet. I've found OliveNation.com in particular to be a reliable resource.

Flaxseeds

Ground flaxseeds make an excellent vegan egg-replacer when combined with water. One tablespoon of the whole seeds produces approximately 1½ tablespoons of the ground powder. While you can purchase pre-ground flax seed meal in many stores, I prefer to grind them fresh for each recipe, as they tend to go rancid much more quickly once broken down. Not to mention, it takes mere seconds to powder your own flax seeds in a spice grinder. If you do opt to purchase flax meal instead, be sure to store the powder in your refrigerator or freezer until you are ready to use it. These tiny seeds can be found in bulk bins and prepackaged in the baking aisle of natural food stores.

Garbanzo Bean (Chickpea) Flour

Gaining in popularity as a versatile gluten-free flour, garbanzo flour is just what you might imagine; nothing but dried, finely ground chickpeas. When used in baking, it can be used as a substitute for about 20%–25% of the wheat flour called for in a recipe or to add a toothsome density to cakes or cookies. It can also be cooked with water like polenta, and eaten either as a hot porridge or let set overnight in a baking dish, sliced, and then fried to make what is called chickpea panisse. Just be warned that eaten raw (if, say, someone decided to sample raw cookie batter that contains garbanzo flour) it is very bitter and unpleasant.

Garbanzo flour should be readily available in most grocery stores in the baking or natural foods section, but if you have a powerful blender like a Vitamix (see Kitchen Toys and Tools) with a dry grinding container, you can make your own from dried, split chickpeas (also known as chana dal). Process 2 cups of legumes at a time, and use the plunger to keep things moving. Once finely ground, let the dust settle for a few minutes before removing the lid of the container.

Graham Crackers

When I first went searching for vegan graham crackers, I was appalled at my lack of options. Why every brand in sight needed to include honey was beyond me. So, what is an intrepid food enthusiast to do in a tight situation like this? Shop, search, and browse some more, of course. Concealed among the rest, and often in natural foods stores, there are a few brands that exclude all animal products. Believe it or not, some of the best options are the store-brand, no-name biscuits that may otherwise get overlooked. Keep your eyes peeled for unexpected steals and deals.

Garlic

Quite possibly the single most celebrated seasoning the world over, garlic itself needs no explanation. Such popularity, however, has given rise to a wide range of garlicky options, some better suited for various recipes than others. There's no standard size for a clove of garlic, but a good rule of thumb is that on average, one will yield about 1 teaspoon, minced. Granulated or powdered garlic is a bit more concentrated, so you can generally substitute ¼–½ teaspoon per clove if you're out of the fresh stuff, or simply want the distinctive flavor without the raw bite. You can also find prepared, already-minced or pureed garlic both in shelf-stable jars and frozen packets for super-speedy cooking needs.

Granulated Sugar

Yes, plain old, regular white sugar. Surprised to see this basic sweetener here? It's true that all sugar (beet or cane) is derived from plant sources and therefore vegan by nature. However, there are some sneaky things going on behind the scenes in big corporations these days. Some cane sugar is filtered using bone char, a very non-vegan process, but that will never be specified on a label. If you're not sure about the brand that you typically buy, your best bet is to contact the manufacturer directly and ask.

To bypass this problem, many vegans purchase unbleached cane sugar. While it is a suitable substitute, unbleached cane sugar does have a higher molasses content than white sugar, so it has more of a brown sugar-like flavor, and tends to produce desserts that are denser. Luckily, there are a few caring companies that go to great pains to ensure the purity of their sugar products, such as Florida Crystals® and Amalgamated Sugar Company®, the suppliers to White Satin, Fred Meyer, Western Family, and Parade. I typically opt for one of these vegan sugar brands to get the best results. You can often find appropriate sugar in health food store bulk bins these days to save some money, but as always, verify the source before forking over the cash. As sugar can be a touchy vegan subject, it is best to use your own judgment when considering which brand to purchase.

Green Pea Flour

Just like garbanzo (or any other bean) flour, green pea flour is the dried and ground powder of its namesake. It's a bit more unusual than most due to its startling color, and it's harder to come by in local markets. Bob's Red Mill® offers it in 24-ounce bags, which will probably last the average cook a lifetime and are readily available on Amazon.com.

Harissa

Many people refer to this as the North African answer to hot sauce, but this complex red pepper paste is so much more sophisticated than that. A wide variety of chilies are blended together, including but not limited to serrano, bell peppers, bird's eye chilies, and dried, rehydrated chilies such as Arbol, Guajillo, chipotle, and ancho peppers, along with more exotic seasonings such as saffron, rosewater, and coriander. This combination lends it an unmistakable, unlimitable spicy perfume. Its closest relative is skhug (otherwise known as shug or zhug), a hot sauce found in Middle Eastern cuisine with similar flavors. You can find jars of harissa either with the other hot sauces at your local specialty market, or among the pickled and preserved foods. Luckily, it's also a snap to make at home from the following formula:

1 Roasted Red Bell Pepper
3–4 Hot Chilies of Choice (See above for suggestions)
4 Cloves Garlic
3 Tablespoons Olive Oil
2 Tablespoons Lemon Juice
1 Teaspoon Salt
½ Teaspoon Ground Caraway
½ Teaspoon Ground Coriander
¼ Teaspoon Ground Cumin
¼ Teaspoon Rosewater
Pinch of Saffron (Optional)

Simply toss all the ingredients into your food processor or blender and pulse to puree, pausing as needed to scrape down the sides of the bowl to make sure everything is incorporated. Once the paste is smooth, transfer to an airtight glass jar and store in the fridge for up to 3 weeks. You can further extend its shelf life if you pour additional oil right on top, just enough to cover the surface and effectively seal the freshness in.

Hemp Seeds

Yes, these are edible seeds from cannabis sativa, but unlike the leaves, they won't get you high. Instead, they're a concentrated source of omega-3 fatty acids and many other vital nutrients, which has bolstered their public profile in recent years. Dubbed a "superfood" by many, what I find most attractive about these tiny kernels is their deeply savory, nutty flavor that blends nicely into both sweet and savory applications. Most hemp seeds are sold hulled, to make them a bit easier on the digestion, and are often squirreled away amongst the dietary supplements or in bulk bins.

Instant Coffee Powder or Granules

Though generally unfit for drinking as intended, instant coffee is an ideal way to add those crave-worthy roasted, smoky notes to any recipe without also incorporating a lot of extra liquid. Stored in a dry, dark place, a small jar should last a long time. You can even find decaf versions, in case you're more sensitive to caffeine but still want that flavor in your recipes. I prefer powder to granules because it dissolves more easily, but both can work interchangeably with a bit of vigorous mixing.

Instant Potato Flakes

Instant mashed potatoes have been a convenient pantry staple since the 1920s when semi-homemade shortcuts were all the rage. Larded with waxy processed fats, dried dairy products, and aggressive doses of salt, these are not the kind of "quick fix" side dishes I can endorse. Rather, I'm looking for just the plain, unadorned flakes of dehydrated potatoes, ready to be reconstituted with hot water and mixed up into any variety of recipe applications. Though rather bland by themselves, that's precisely what makes them so versatile. You're more likely to encounter them in health food stores or online shops, either in large packages or bulk bins. Just make sure there's nothing else added, and that they are in fact flakes, not granules, since the two formats absorb liquid at a different rate.

Instant Wakame Flakes

Is it strange to profess your love for a seaweed? If it is, well, I never claimed I was normal. Instant wakame flakes are a constant staple in my pantry, dried and indefinitely shelf-stable, but ready to rehydrate in a minute or less. Their flavor is relatively mild, compared to other oceanic vegetables; the spinach of the sea, as I like to call it. Plus, the short strips are tender and very easy to eat, be it in soups, salads, stir-fry, or seasoned rice. You can find inexpensive packets in Japanese markets or online via Amazon.com.

Jackfruit

Practically unheard of just a few years ago, jackfruit has taken the world by storm for its uncanny ability to imitate the texture of shredded meat. These tropical fruits can grow to gigantic proportions, easily exceeding 80 pounds, and their spiny exterior makes them quite a sight to behold. You're much more likely to encounter them canned, which is a merciful thing because their latex-y interior is a real pain to break down, coating everything from your knife to your hands in stubbornly sticky goo. Always make sure you're purchasing young (or "immature") green jackfruit in brine, NOT in syrup. The sweetened stuff is objectively dreadful.

Kelp Powder

The term "kelp" covers a large family of sea vegetables also known as brown algae, all boasting impressive amounts of iodine, iron, and a whole battery of additional vitamins and minerals that make them some of the most mineral-dense foods in the world. Dried and ground to a fine powder, they're generally intended to be taken as a medicinal supplement. Most people put them into capsules to get past the naturally fishy flavor, but I've found that an invaluable addition to faux-seafood preparations. Sometimes the grind can be on the coarse side, so pass the powder through a fine mesh sieve if you're particularly texture-sensitive.

Maple Syrup

One of my absolute favorite sweeteners, there is simply no substitute for real, 100% maple syrup. The flavor is like nothing else out there, and I have yet to meet a single brand of pancake syrup that could even come close. Of course, this incredible indulgence does come at a hefty price. Though it would be absolute sacrilege to use anything but authentic Grade B maple syrup on pancakes or waffles in my house, I will sometimes bend the rules in recipes where it isn't such a prominent flavor, in order to save some money. In these instances, I'll substitute with a maple-agave blend, which still carries the flavor from the actual source, but bulks it up with an equal dose of agave for sweetening power. Grade A is a fine substitute in a pinch, but contrary to what the letter would suggest, it's actually less flavorful than Grade B.

Matcha

Perhaps one of my all-time favorite flavorings, matcha is a very high-quality powdered green tea. It is used primarily in Japanese tea ceremonies and can have an intense, complex, and bitter taste when used in large amounts. Contrary to what many new bakers think, this is NOT the same as the green tea leaves you'll find in mega mart tea bags! Those are vastly inferior in the flavor department, and real matcha is ground much finer. There are many levels of quality, with each step up in grade carrying a higher price tag. Because it can become quite pricey, I would suggest buying a mid-range or "culinary" grade, which should be readily available at any specialty tea store and many health food markets.

Miso Paste

Fermented soybeans coarsely ground and mixed with water sounds like a sad excuse for soup, yet it's the single most celebrated starter for any Japanese meal, be it breakfast, lunch, or dinner. The length of time that the beans are fermented determines the color and flavor of the finished paste; traditional miso is aged for at least 3–5 years, yielding a very dark, robust, and salty base. Lighter, gentler miso is often called "sweet" miso, which is delicious used as a condiment as well, spread very thinly on an ear of roasted corn, for example. Those sensitive to soy can now find many alternatives as well, the most common being chickpea miso, which more closely mimics the flavor of a light or white miso paste. Though all types can be substituted with more or less success, no two misos are exactly alike, and any changes can drastically change the end results.

Mochiko

Mochiko is simply finely ground mochi flour, or glutinous rice flour. You can find this in any Asian specialty market or online. Koda Farms® is one of the most common brands available in the US; it can be purchased in compact, white 1-pound boxes.

Nondairy Milk

The foundation of many cream and custard pies, I kept this critical ingredient somewhat ambiguous for a reason. Most types of nondairy milk will work in these recipes, which leaves the possibilities wide open for anyone that needs to accommodate allergies or intolerances. Unless explicitly specified, any other type of vegan milk-substitute will work. My top pick is unsweetened almond milk because it tends to be a bit thicker, richer, and still has a neutral flavor. Don't be afraid to experiment, though; there's a lot to choose from!

Nori

If you've ever eaten sushi, you're already well acquainted with nori. It's the flat sheet of seaweed wrapped around your rice, so dark green that sometimes it looks black. Nori is easily found in any grocery store that has a section devoted to Asian imports, and most options are equally suitable for all preparations. The whole sheets work well as low-carb wraps beyond the sushi sphere, but they can also be snipped or crumbled into oceanic toppings for ramen, soba noodles, or rice bowls.

Nutritional Yeast

Unlike active yeast, nutritional yeast is not used to leaven baked goods, but to flavor all sorts of dishes. Prized for its distinctly cheesy flavor, it's a staple in most vegan pantries and is finally starting to gain recognition in mainstream cooking as well. Though almost always found in savory recipes, I sometimes like to add a tiny pinch to some desserts, bringing out its subtle buttery characteristics. It can be found either in the baking aisle or in many bulk bin sections.

Panko Bread Crumbs

This Japanese import is much crisper and more airy than so-called "Italian-style" bread crumbs. That unique texture allows it to better resist absorbing oil when fried, yielding lighter, less greasy coatings. When used as filler or binder within recipes, it has a less prominent wheat flavor, allowing it to blend seamlessly into the background of just about anything, sweet or savory.

Salt

The importance of salt cannot be overstated. It's that spark that makes flavors pop and balances out spice mixtures that might otherwise overwhelm the palate. To make a long story short, you do not want to leave out this unassuming but critical ingredient! Unless otherwise noted, I use regular old table salt (finely ground) in baking. Flaky sea salt or kosher salt can be fun to sprinkle directly over finished baked goods before serving for an extra punch of flavor, but be careful not to overdo it; there's a fine line between salted and downright salty.

Seitan

All hail seitan! No, there's no demon worship going on here, and in fact seitan originated on the opposite end of that spectrum. Buddhist monks first invented this "wheat meat" in ancient China, long before there was even a word for vegetarianism. Seitan is pure gluten, the stuff of celiac nightmares, but of body building dreams. Ounce for ounce, seitan has the same amount of protein as lean ground beef, and of course, less fat and no cholesterol. Textures range from chewy to spongy to pleasantly sinewy, depending on how it's sliced and cooked. Ready to use, prepared seitan can be found in health food stores and Whole Foods Markets alongside the packages of refrigerated tofu.

Sour Cream

Another creative alternative comes to the rescue of vegan eaters everywhere! Vegan sour cream provides an amazingly similar yet dairy-free version of the original tangy spread. In a pinch, I suppose you might be able to get away with using soy yogurt instead, but that is generally much thinner, so I really wouldn't recommend it. Vegan sour cream is sold in the refrigerated section of natural food stores and some mainstream grocers. It can often be found neatly tucked in among its dairy-based rivals, or with the other refrigerated dairy alternatives.

Speculoos

Crisp like gingersnaps but redolent of cinnamon rather than ginger, these brown sugar cookies can be spiced heavily or lightly, rolled thick or thin, and used as an ingredient or finished treat by themselves. No two bakers' speculoos will taste the same, but Biscoff by Lotus® brand has set the standard with a mild, universally beloved cookie that is perfectly engineered for dipping into a cup of steaming coffee or hot chocolate. Lacking access to this crisp Belgian treat, graham crackers sprinkled with a bit of cinnamon can suffice in a pinch.

Sprinkles

What's a birthday party without a generous handful of sprinkles to brighten up the cake? Though these colorful toppers are made primarily of edible wax, they are often coated in confectioner's glaze, which is code for mashed up insects, to give them their lustrous shine. Happily, you can now find specifically vegan sprinkles (sold as "sprinkelz") produced by the Let's Do…® company, in both chocolate and colored versions, which can be found at just about any natural food store.

Sriracha

True heat-seekers and hot sauce fanatics may scoff at the relatively mild spice of sriracha, but that very quality is what makes it such a winning condiment for enhancing all cuisines. Leaning more heavily on garlic and a balanced sweetness than just pure fire power, it's dangerously easy to power through even the largest bottles available. Don't hold back, just enjoy the blaze; it's dirt-cheap and found literally everywhere, even in gas stations and truck stops.

Sumac

Ask the Internet what it thinks about "sumac" and the first thing to pop up won't be about its culinary value, but about its toxicity. While closely related to poison ivy and sometimes confused with its less friendly brethren in the wild, dried and ground sumac is an entirely different beast. Contributing the pucker-power of a lemon with punchy sourness and astringency, it has the benefit of being a powdered seasoning that won't water down your dishes. For a reasonable stand-in, blend lemon zest with a pinch of salt, but don't expect the exact same results.

Tahini

An irreplaceable staple in Middle Eastern cuisine, most regular grocery stores should be able to accommodate your tahini requests. Tahini is a paste very much like peanut butter, but made from sesame seeds rather than nuts. If you don't have any on hand and a trip to the market is not in your immediate plans, then any other nut butter will provide the same texture within a recipe, though it will impart a different overall taste. You can also make your own, just like you would make nut butter, but a high-speed blender is highly recommended to achieve a smooth texture.

Tamarind Paste

Tangy, tart, and often downright sour, tamarind possesses a powerful, sometimes polarizing flavor that's best used sparingly to balance out a dish, rather than dominate. Harvesting the edible fruit from the pod can be a taxing proposition, thanks to its tough outer shell, fibrous interior, and hard, sticky seeds. Head straight for the prepared paste, a smooth, soft puree, to bypass the labor without sacrificing the taste. It's readily available anywhere that exotic fruits are sold, either in the fresh produce section or canned goods aisle. Stored in an airtight container in the fridge, I've found that it's pretty much indestructible.

Tempeh

Tempeh is often compared to tofu because it's another high-protein soy product, but that's pretty much where the similarities end. Much more strongly flavored than tofu, tempeh is made from whole beans, and sometimes grains and even seeds, which are bound together in a fermented cake. Good bacteria cultures like those found in yogurt are the catalyst for this slow transformation, which makes it particularly high in B12 and beneficial for gut health. Raw tempeh can be somewhat bitter which is why it's best cooked over high heat with equally assertive marinades. Although there are many different varieties available, they can all be used interchangeably.

Tofu

No longer the poster child for flavorless vegetarian cookery, tofu is enjoying greater acceptance than ever as a highly versatile protein in its own right, rather than merely a bland meat substitute. For entrees where the tofu is chopped, sliced or cubed, you should seek out firm, extra-firm, or even super-firm, water-packed varieties than can hold their own when the heat is on. Medium or firm are better for crumbled applications, and soft or silken is most appropriate for creamy purees, such as sauces, smoothies, and puddings. When I use tofu for baked goods and ice creams, I always reach for the aseptic, shelf stable packs. Not only do they seem to last forever when unopened, but they also blend down into a perfectly smooth liquid when processed thoroughly, not a trace of grit or off-flavors to be found. Water-packed varieties can be stored for up to a month unopened, or 1 week if stored in an airtight container in the fridge, covered in fresh water that's changed every 2 or 3 days.

Vanilla (Extract, Paste, and Beans)

One of the most important ingredients in a baker's arsenal, vanilla is found in countless forms and qualities. It goes without saying that artificial flavorings pale in comparison to the real thing. Madagascar vanilla is the traditional full-bodied vanilla that most people appreciate in desserts, so stick with that and you can't go wrong. Happily, it's also the most common and moderately priced variety. To take your desserts up a step, vanilla paste brings in the same amount of flavor, but includes those lovely little vanilla bean flecks that makes everyone think you busted out the good stuff and used whole beans. Vanilla paste can be substituted 1:1 for vanilla extract. Like whole vanilla beans, save the paste for things where you'll really see those specks of vanilla goodness, like ice creams, custards, and frostings. Vanilla beans, the most costly but flavorful option, can be used instead, at about 1 bean per 2 teaspoons of extract or paste.

Once you've split and scraped out the insides, don't toss that vanilla pod! Get the most for your money by stashing it in a container of granulated sugar, to slowly infuse the sugar with delicious vanilla flavor. Alternately, just store the pod in a container until it dries out, and then grind it up very finely in a high-speed blender and use it to augment a good vanilla extract. The flavor won't be nearly as strong as the seeds, but it does contribute to the illusion that you've used the good stuff.

Vegetable Stock

Be it brothy or creamy, thick or thin, a soup is only as good as its stock. Stock can be made up of absolutely any vegetables, but the most common ingredients are onions, carrots, and celery, at bare minimum. The trouble with commercial, ready-made options are that most lean too heavily on salt, throwing the carefully balanced seasoning of a dish out of whack. Always seek out low-sodium or no salted added varieties whenever possible, and read labels carefully to avoid artificial flavorings or preservatives. My favorite pantry staple is actual dry vegetable stock powder, which can be added to water according to taste. The best vegetable stock will always be homemade, though. If you have some extra time and some scraps, it's effortless to whip up and then freeze for later use. These aren't set rules, only guidelines, so never feel constrained to any particular measurements if you come up shy or just want to experiment.

Basic Vegetable Stock Blueprint

2 Cups Chopped Alliums (Onions, Shallot, Leeks, and/or Scallions)
2 Cups Chopped Root Vegetables (Carrots, Sweet Potatoes, and/or Turnips)
1 Cup Chopped Celery or Fennel
1 Bay Leaf
1 Teaspoon Whole Black Peppercorns
Salt, to Taste
Additional Options: Garlic, Pumpkin, Tomatoes, Mushrooms, Fresh Parsley, Dried Thyme, Turmeric

Toss all the ingredients, except for the salt, into a large stock pot, and add just enough water to cover the vegetables. Bring to a boil, cover, and then turn down the heat to keep the liquid at a gentle simmer. Let cook for anywhere between 1–2 hours, bearing in mind that the longer you can wait, the more flavor you can extract. Strain out the vegetable solids, saving them either for a puree, soup, or simply compost, and season the golden-brown stock with salt, to taste. Use right away or let cool, transfer into airtight containers, and store in either the fridge or freezer. The stock will keep for up to a week in the fridge, and for up to 4 months in the freezer.

Vinegar

At any given time, there are at least five different types of vinegar kicking around my kitchen, and that's a conservative estimate. As with oil, vinegar can be made from all sorts of fruit, grains, and roots, each with their own distinctive twang. Some, like white vinegar, rice vinegar, and apple cider vinegar are fairly neutral and mild, others like balsamic vinegar and red wine vinegar are far more assertive. The type you choose can radically change the character of the finished dish, which is why they all have a place in my pantry. Feel free to experiment with different varieties for a change of pace if you're open to new flavor adventures. In a pinch, you might also be able to get away with using fresh lemon or lime juice for a similar acidic punch.

Wasabi Paste and Powder

Just like the mounds of green paste served with sushi, the prepared wasabi paste found in tubes is almost certainly not made of wasabi root. Strange but true, it's typically colored horseradish instead, due to the rarity and expense of real wasabi. Read labels carefully, because it's one of those things that seems guaranteed to be vegan-friendly, but can give you a nasty surprise if you're not careful. Milk derivatives are often added, for reasons I couldn't begin to explain. Wasabi powder can be potent stuff indeed, but only if it's extremely fresh. The flavor dissipates over time, so be sure to toss any that has been sitting in your pantry well past its prime. If quality paste is nowhere to be found, opt for prepared horseradish (blended only with a dash of vinegar) instead. In some cases, mustard powder can lend a similar flavor instead of wasabi powder, but only in very small doses.

Whipped Cream

Still something of a novelty, ready-to-use aerosol cans of vegan whipped "cream" do exist in Whole Foods Markets and many specialty health food stores. Made by Soyatoo®, it can be found in both rice- and soy-based versions, and sprays out fluffy and lightly sweetened every time. So Delicious® recently unleashed a frozen whipped topping alternative as well, which needs only to thaw in the fridge before it can be generously dolloped on all manner of sweet treats. Unfortunately, these toppings are still not widely available, so it's much more practical and nearly as easy to make your own from scratch. All you need is a can of full-fat coconut milk and a bit of patience. Place the whole, unopened can in the fridge and let it chill for at least 3 hours. This will allow the cream to rise to the top and solidify, which you can then skim off in thick spoonfuls. Leave the watery refuse behind for another recipe (it's great in curries and soups!) Place the coconut cream in the bowl of your stand mixer, and whip vigorously for 5–8 minutes, until thick, fluffy, and luscious. Sprinkle in a touch of sugar and a few drops of vanilla extract, if desired.

White Whole Wheat Flour

Move over, whole wheat pastry flour, healthy bakers everywhere have a new best friend! It may look and taste like regular white flour, but it's actually milled from the whole grain. Simply made from hard white wheat berries instead of red, the color and flavor is much lighter, making it the perfect addition to nearly every sort of baking application you can think of. If you're concerned about getting more fiber into your diet, feel free to switch out the all-purpose flour in any recipe in this book for white whole wheat.

Wine

While I don't often drink, I can tell you that if your wine isn't something you'd want in a glass, it's not something you'd want to cook or bake with, either. Avoid so-called "cooking wines" and just go with something moderately priced, and on the drier side for a savory dish or something a bit sweeter to complement a dessert. Don't be afraid to ask for help when you go shopping; the people who work at wine stores tend to have good advice about these things! Be vigilant and do your homework though, because not all wines are vegan. Shockingly, some are filtered through isinglass, which is made from fish bladders. To avoid a fishy brew, double check brands on Barnivore.com.

Wonton Wrappers

Little more than flour and water, traditional wonton wrappers would never raise the alarm for those of a vegan disposition, but modern manufacturing has roped preservatives and other additives into the equation. Read labels carefully to double-check for eggs or any of their individual components, and you should be in the clear. There are all sizes and shapes of wonton wrappers available, both fresh and frozen, typically nearby the water-packed tofu in the produce department.

Yogurt

Fermented by good bacteria that are said to improve your digestion, yogurt now comes in just about any flavor, color, or nondairy formulation you can imagine. Soy, almond, coconut, and even cashew yogurts are readily available at most markets these days, and you can even find some that are agave-sweetened, too. Just double-check that whatever you decide to buy is certified as vegan; just because it's nondairy doesn't mean it uses vegan cultures. The big, multi-serving tubs are handy if you eat a lot of the stuff to begin with, but I generally prefer to purchase single-serving, 6-ounce containers for specific uses to avoid leftovers that may go bad too soon. Please note, however, that one container of yogurt does not equal one cup; 6 ounces will be equivalent to about ¾ cup by volume measure. It does help to have a food scale if you decide to buy in bulk to weigh out the exact amount that would be found in one standard container.

Young Thai Coconuts

Just as the name might suggest, young Thai coconuts are sold earlier than the iconic brown-husked versions. The white shell on these immature fruits is much easier to penetrate with your kitchen knife and a few solid whacks, revealing a generous pool of sweet water and soft flesh within. The "meat" is easily scooped out with a sturdy spoon and typically enjoyed raw. Young Thai coconuts are found refrigerated in the produce section of many health food stores, but you can find much better deals at any Asian market.

Yuba

If you've ever made pudding and discovered a thin skin has formed on the surface once cooled, you're already well versed in the ways of yuba. Large vats of soymilk are cooked slowly, allowing the proteins to coagulate and rise to the top, knitting themselves into a thin matrix of silky, gossamer-thin tofu that can be skimmed off in sheets. A delicacy with a short shelf life, it can be difficult to find fresh yuba in many parts of the country, but you might have better luck hunting through the freezer aisles of Asian grocery stores. Yuba can also be dried and later rehydrated in hot water, although the flavor and texture really can't compare.

Conversions and Equivalents

US Dry Volume Measurements

MEASURE	EQUIVALENT
⅟₁₆ Teaspoon	Dash
⅛ Teaspoon	Pinch
3 Teaspoons	1 Tablespoon
⅛ Cup	2 Tablespoons (Also Equivalent to 1 Standard Coffee Scoop)
¼ Cup	4 Tablespoons
⅓ Cup	5 Tablespoons + 1 Teaspoon
½ Cup	8 Tablespoons
¾ Cup	12 Tablespoons
1 Cup	16 Tablespoons
1 Pound	16 Ounces

US Liquid Volume Measurements

8 Fluid Ounces	1 Cup
1 Pint	2 Cups (16 Fluid Ounces)
1 Quart	2 Pints (4 Cups)
1 Gallon	4 Quarts (16 Cups)

US to Metric Conversions

⅕ Teaspoon	1 ml (ml stands for milliliter; one thousandth of a liter)
1 Teaspoon	5 ml
1 Tablespoon	15 ml
1 Fluid Ounce	30 ml
⅕ Cup	50 ml
1 Cup	240 ml
2 Cups (1 Pint)	470 ml

4 Cups (1 Quart)	.95 liter
4 Quarts (1 Gallon)	3.8 liters
1 Ounce	28 grams
1 Pound	454 grams

Metric to US Conversions

1 ml	⅕ Teaspoon
5 ml	1 Teaspoon
15 ml	1 Tablespoon
30 ml	1 Fluid Ounces
100 ml	3.4 Fluid Ounces
240 ml	1 Cup
1 liter	34 Fluid Ounces
1 liter	4.2 Cups
1 liter	2.1 Pints
1 liter	1.06 Quarts
1 liter	.26 Gallon
1 gram	.035 Ounce
100 grams	3.5 Ounces
500 grams	1.1 Pounds
1 kilogram	2.205 Pounds
1 kilogram	35 Ounces

Measures for Pans and Dishes

9x13-inch baking dish	22x33-centimeter baking dish
8x8-inch baking dish	20x20-centimeter baking dish
9x5-inch loaf pan	23x12-centimeter loaf pan (=8 cups or 2 liters in capacity)
10-inch tart or cake pan	25-centimeter tart or cake pan
9-inch cake pan	22-centimeter cake pan

Oven Temperature Conversions

Fahrenheit	Celsius	Gas Mark
275°F	140°C	gas mark 1–cool
300°F	150°C	gas mark 2
325°F	165°C	gas mark 3–very moderate
350°F	180°C	gas mark 4–moderate
375°F	190°C	gas mark 5
400°F	200°C	gas mark 6–moderately hot
425°F	220°C	gas mark 7–hot
450°F	230°C	gas mark 9
475°F	240°C	gas mark 10–very hot

Ratios for Selected Foods

Butter

1 stick	4 Ounces (113 grams)	8 Tablespoons	½ Cup
4 sticks	16 Ounces (452 grams)	32 Tablespoons	2 Cups

Lemon

1 Lemon	1–3 Tablespoons Juice	1–1½ Teaspoons Zest
4 Lemons	1 Cup Juice	¼ Cup Zest

Chocolate

1 Ounce	¼ Cup Finely Grated (40 grams)
6 Ounces Chips	1 Cup Chips (160 grams)
Cocoa Powder	1 Cup (115 grams)

BREAKFAST

A+ Benedicts

Makes 4 Servings

Twists on the beloved eggs benedict are as diverse as the eaters that happily eat them up, but this particularly green tower of plant-based breakfast delights will surely rise to the head of the class. Top marks go to its star ingredients: avocado, asparagus, and arugula. A smart trio that freshens up the typically meat-heavy affair, smoky stalks of tender-crisp asparagus take the place of bacon, while rich avocado hollandaise sauce adds a certain decadence that could make butter blush. Offset by the pepper bite of arugula, slabs of protein-packed tofu take on the unmistakable essence of boiled eggs, given away only by their unmistakable rectangular shape.

Bringing together such a masterpiece early in the morning may seem like a complex equation, but each individual component is ingeniously designed for maximum efficiency. If the first meal of the day ever tests your patience, bust out this brilliant formula for a guaranteed high score.

Start by preparing the eggless tofu patties. Take your tofu slices and blot them lightly with paper towels to remove a bit of the excess moisture on the surface. Combine the nutritional yeast, onion powder, black salt, turmeric, and pepper in a small dish, and dredge the tofu in the mixture, coating all sides as thoroughly as possible.

Place a large skillet on the stove over medium-high heat. Add the oil and once shimmering, gently add the slices of tofu in one even layer, making sure that all pieces make full contact with the bottom of the pan. Cook for 2 minutes without moving them, and then flip, cooking for another minute or two on the opposite side, until lightly golden around the edges. You're not looking for a hard sear here, but a tender crust that will help the seasoning to stay put. Remove the patties and set them aside.

Meanwhile, quickly throw together the hollandaise by simply tossing all the ingredients, except for the oil, into your blender or food processor. Puree on high speed, pausing as needed to incorporate everything into a smooth blend. Slowly drizzle in the oil with the motor running to fully emulsify the mixture.

Once the tofu is out of the pan, tap out any browned pieces of crust that might remain and return the pan to the stove. Sauté

Tofu Egg Patties:

- 1 (14-Ounce Package) Firm Tofu, Drained and Cut Crosswise into 8 Slices
- 3 Tablespoons Nutritional Yeast
- 1 Teaspoon Onion Powder
- 1 Teaspoon Black Salt (Kala Namak)
- ½ Teaspoon Ground Turmeric
- ⅛ Teaspoon Ground Black Pepper
- 2 Tablespoons Olive Oil

Avocado Hollandaise Sauce:

- 1 Medium Ripe Avocado
- 2 Tablespoons Lemon Juice
- 1 Teaspoon Dijon Mustard
- 1 Teaspoon Apple Cider Vinegar
- ¼ Teaspoon Salt
- ¼ Cup Avocado Oil or Olive Oil

Continued on next page

the asparagus in olive oil for a minute before adding in all the remaining liquid ingredients at once. Stir thoroughly to combine, tossing the asparagus to coat. Continue stirring periodically until the vegetables are bright green and fork-tender. There may still be some excess marinade that hasn't fully absorbed; drain if necessary.

To assemble, place two halves of toasted English muffin on each plate and top each with a handful of arugula. Place a tofu egg patty on top next, followed by a layer of smoky asparagus, lining up as many stalks as will comfortably fit in a row. Finish the whole thing with a generous spoonful of avocado hollandaise sauce and a pinch of freshly chopped parsley, if desired.

Smoky Asparagus:

- ½ Pound Asparagus, Trimmed, Halved Lengthwise, and Cut into Approximately 2-Inch Pieces
- 2 Tablespoons Olive Oil
- 1 Tablespoon Soy Sauce
- 1 Teaspoon Maple Syrup
- 1 Teaspoon Balsamic Vinegar
- 1 Teaspoon Liquid Smoke

For Assembly:

- 4 English Muffins, Split and Toasted
- 3–4 Ounces Baby Arugula
- ¼ Cup Fresh Parsley, Finely Chopped (Optional)

Chia Seed Congee

MAKES 2–4 SERVINGS

Savory oatmeal, revitalized by glamorous beauty shots on social media and effusive praise by foodies, has been embraced by western society like never before. The concept is far from new, however, as a sweet morning start is much less common for most early risers around the globe. Riffing off that same melody, you'll find a wide range of warm grain dishes that will help start your day off on the right food, such as the creamy rice-based congee popular in China and the surrounding vicinity. Rice, be it basmati, brown, or anything in between, takes longer to cook than plain oats, but the instant varieties lose a bit of their textural appeal in such a cereal-focused application. Chia seeds, on the other hand, plump up almost instantly in any sort of liquid environment, lending a unique tapioca-like viscosity to any flavorful base.

Always seeking to please, these nutritional powerhouses can transition from savory to sweet, accommodating your every whim upon waking. Consider both varieties as just a baseline to build upon; take stock of your pantry and swap in any nuts, fruits (dried or fresh), and seasonings on hand to make your bowl all your own.

Continued on page 39

The basic procedure for both sweet and savory congee is the same. Place the chia seeds in a small saucepan along with the liquid (either vegetable stock or non-dairy milk) and whisk vigorously to break up any clumps. The seeds will want to stick together, so make sure you keep whisking as the mixture cooks. Add in the seasonings and aromatics—the soy sauce, garlic, ginger, and white pepper in the case of the savory version, and the maple syrup, ginger, and cinnamon for the sweet. Cook over medium-high heat for 5–8 minutes, until thick and creamy. Either fold in the remaining goodies for your chosen flavor adventure or ladle the mixture into bowls first and sprinkle them artfully on top. Enjoy right away, while hot and steamy.

Should you get stuck in a congee rut, here are a few additional topping ideas I've come to know and love:

Savory:
Sliced Avocado
Vegan Kimchi
Diced or Sliced Smoked
    Tofu
Sriracha or Chile Oil

Sweet:
Crystalized Ginger
Sliced Bananas
Peanut Butter
Jam or Fruit Preserves

SAVORY CONGEE:

½ Cup White Chia Seeds*
2½ Cups Vegetable Stock
2 Teaspoons Soy Sauce
1 Clove Garlic, Minced
1 Teaspoon Minced Fresh
    Ginger
¼ Teaspoon Ground White
    Pepper
1 Fresh Shiitake Mushroom,
    Stemmed and Sliced
4 Scallions
½ Cup Shelled Edamame
¼ Cup Toasted Cashews

SWEET CONGEE:

½ Cup White Chia Seeds*
2½ Cups Plain Nondairy Milk
2 Tablespoons 100% Grade B
    Maple Syrup
½ Teaspoon Minced Fresh
    Ginger
½ Teaspoon Ground
    Cinnamon
2–4 Medjool Dates, Pitted
    and Sliced
½ Cup Cooked Adzuki Beans
¼ Cup Goji Berries or Golden
    Raisins
2 Tablespoons Toasted
    Sesame Seeds

*Black chia seeds taste and work just as well, but may not be quite as visually appealing.

Cake Batter Breakfast Bars

MAKES 6–8 BARS

Cake: It's what's for breakfast. When you wake up craving something sweet, you no longer need to curb the impulse to eat dessert first, thanks to these superlative, satisfying bars. The protein-rich base boasts a vibrant rainbow of sprinkles, nuts, and chocolates, right alongside a powerful dose of vital nutrients to help you power through the morning. Soft and chewy, with a hearty crunch in every bite, don't even call them "protein bars" when you should just call them "delicious."

Line an 8x4–inch loaf pan with aluminum foil, lightly grease, and set aside.

In the bowl of your stand mixer, combine 1 cup of the protein powder, oat flour and salt. You can also mix everything by hand in a large bowl, but the batter is very thick and difficult to stir, so you'll need to put some serious muscle into it. Be prepared to ditch the spatula and use your hands towards the end, too!

Separately, mix together the cashew butter, melted coconut oil, agave, and vanilla before adding the whole concoction into the bowl of dry goods. Begin to mix slowly to incorporate. After about a minute of stirring, add in the sprinkles, nuts, and/or chocolate, in any proportion your heart desires, as long as it's no more than ½ cup in total.

If the batter still seems too soft to handle, add in the remaining ¼ cup of protein powder. Once smooth, cohesive, and approximately the texture of moldable clay, transfer the dough to your prepared pan and smooth it down into an even layer. Place the pan in the freezer for at least 5–6 minutes, just until the bars are firm enough to cut. Use the foil like a sling to pull the bars out, and slice into individual servings. Store in an airtight container or wrapped in plastic in the fridge.

- 1–1¼ Cups Vanilla Rice or Pea Protein Powder
- ½ Cup Oat Flour
- ¼ Teaspoon Salt
- ⅓ Cup Raw Cashew Butter
- ¼ Cup Coconut Oil, Melted
- ¼ Cup Light Agave Nectar
- 1 Teaspoon Vanilla Extract
- ½ Cup Sprinkles, Chopped Nuts, and/or Mini Chocolate Chips

Hash Brown Waffles

MAKES 4 WAFFLES

Little more than piles of shredded potatoes, what separates superlative hash browns from the merely adequate hash browns all comes down to texture. Shatteringly crisp on the outside yet tender, even borderline creamy on the inside, it's a fine balance that's difficult to strike. Using a waffle iron instead of a standard frying pan maximizes the surface contact for a far more satisfying crunchy crust, while the enclosure allows the spuds to essentially steam from within, ensuring perfectly tender bites through and through.

Before doing anything else, begin preheating your waffle iron. All models work differently so yours may take more or less time to reach a suitable temperature.

Squeeze any excess water out of the shredded potatoes if necessary before tossing them into a large bowl. Mix in the melted vegan butter or oil, salt, and pepper, stirring thoroughly to incorporate. Make sure that the shreds are all evenly coated before proceeding.

Lightly grease the waffle maker. Distribute the potato mixture equally between four waffle squares, covering the surface as evenly as possible while packing it in firmly. Close the lid and make sure that it locks to ensure full contact with the hash browns. Cook on medium-high for 5–8 minutes, until golden brown all over. Serve right away, while still hot and crisp!

1 Pound Frozen Shredded Potatoes,* Thawed

1½ Tablespoons Vegan Butter or Coconut Oil, Melted

½ Teaspoon Salt

¼ Teaspoon Ground Black Pepper

*You can also find ready-to-cook shredded potatoes in the refrigerated sections of some grocery stores, alongside prepared and packaged side dishes.

Quick Tip: When time is of the essence, don't waffle around. Just toss the mixture into a large skillet and fry the mixture over medium-high heat to make more traditional hash brown potatoes.

Spice It Up! Honey-butter potato chips are a craze sweeping Asian nations and are slowly catching on overseas. Taking a page from that addictive sweet and salty combination, I love adding 1½ tablespoons dark amber agave and ⅛ teaspoon orange blossom water or rose water to mimic that ambrosial, subtly floral flavor.

Mo-Chata Pancakes

MAKES 6–8 PANCAKES; 2 SERVINGS

All I wanted was a cinnamon-flecked pancake made with rice flour to evoke the flavors of horchata, Latin America's most refreshing iced nondairy drink, but an accidental ingredient swap in the bulk bin section led me to an all new sort of cultural fusion. Cooking up beautifully, tender and evenly amber, my mistake became clear only when I went in for a bite. The texture was chewy, not fluffy, and I realized I had grabbed glutinous rice flour, rather than plain white. I had inadvertently invented horchata-flavored mochi pancakes; mo-chata! Disappointed at first, I began plotting a second attempt after another trip to the grocery store, all the while munching on my "failure." When suddenly the whole batch was gone, I still wanted to make another one . . . but without any changes whatsoever. Though not what I had initially envisioned, they turned out to be something even better.

Whisk both flours, cinnamon, baking powder and soda, and salt together into a bowl, making sure that all the dry goods are equally distributed throughout. Separately, mix together the nondairy milk, agave, oil, and vinegar. Pour the liquid ingredients into the bowl of dry, whisking vigorously until the batter is smooth. A few small lumps are fine to leave in the mix, so there's no need to go too crazy.

Meanwhile, lightly grease a large nonstick skillet or griddle over medium heat on the stove. When hot, ladle out a scant ¼ cup or so of the batter for each pancake, forming rounds approximately 3–4 inches in diameter. Give the pancakes enough space that you can easy maneuver a spatula underneath and flip them. Cook for 3–4 minutes on each side, flipping once the underside is golden brown and bubbles have burst on top. If you can't cook all the pancakes at once, repeat as necessary.

Top with sliced almonds, a sprinkle of additional cinnamon, confectioner's sugar, or a drizzle of good old maple syrup.

¾ Cup Glutinous White Rice Flour (Mochiko)

¼ Cup All-Purpose Flour

1 Teaspoon Ground Cinnamon

1½ Teaspoons Baking Powder

¼ Teaspoon Baking Soda

¼ Teaspoon Salt

¾ Cup Plain Nondairy Milk

1 Tablespoon Light Agave Nectar

1 Tablespoon Olive Oil

½ Teaspoon Apple Cider Vinegar

Papaya Boats

MAKES 1–2 SERVINGS

Seeking a tropical escape from the everyday banality of the usual breakfast suspects, one need look no further than the papaya for inspiration. Orange- and pink-hued fruits, more brilliant than a sunrise in paradise, are hollowed out to form unsinkable boats stuffed to the brim with yogurt and all the toppings your heart desires. Contrast is essential for maximum satisfaction, so a variety of seeds and crunchy garnishes always make the cut on my sweet life rafts. Consider the following more of a guideline than a recipe. Sail away to new adventures with this fruity foundation!

Slice the papaya in half lengthwise and scoop out the seeds. Discard or save them for another recipe (they're great as a peppery addition to salad dressings!).

Spoon the yogurt into the two halves, dividing it equally between them. Top with the fresh fruits, nuts, and seeds, and finish with a drizzle of agave if you prefer your breakfast on the sweeter side.

- 1 Medium Ripe Papaya
- 1 Cup Vanilla Vegan Yogurt
- 2 Kiwis, Peeled and Sliced
- ½ Cup Blueberries
- ¼ Cup Toasted Coconut Chips
- 2 Tablespoons Hemp Seeds
- 1 Tablespoon Amber Agave Nectar (Optional)

Quick Tip: If you're in a real rush, skip all the slicing and dicing; top the yogurt-filled papaya with a handful of your favorite granola on top, grab a spoon, and go to town.

Switch it up! Anything goes here, so don't be afraid to mix up the topping based on your tastes, or simply what's kicking around in the pantry. Pepitas, sunflower seeds, chia seeds, macadamia nuts, walnuts, or puffed cereal can all add a satisfying crunch. Explore other fruity flavors with fresh berries, sliced bananas, or dried cranberries, just for starters. Dress it up for a more decadent treat, too. Dish out a few scoops of ice cream instead of yogurt, and you'll have a breezy island-inspired dessert on your hands.

Pumpkin Spice Latte French Toast

MAKES 4 SERVINGS

Before the first leaves turn red or birds begin to fly south, the arrival of pumpkin-spiced everything heralds the coming of fall. Now synonymous with the season, it's infused into absolutely everything edible, drinkable, smell-able, and visible. Nothing is immune from the powers of pumpkin spice, and much as I try to fight it, the allure is undeniable. Although the hype is drastically overblown, it still has genuine culinary merit, and is more than welcome on my breakfast table—but not in my coffee. Lattes aren't my first pick for this flavor; rather, it turns up in more full-bodied mealtime fare, such as thick slices of custardy French toast. Like sponges built to absorb sweetness and spice, they carry the theme far better than any thin liquid spiked with artificial additives. Plus, unlike your average latte, you can actually taste the pumpkin, not just a hit of pure sugar.

It's ideal if you can start with either slightly stale or lightly toasted bread, since it will be a bit firmer and hold up better to the extra moisture that you'll be adding.

Combine the sugar, coffee powder, spices, and salt in a shallow pan, making sure that all the seasonings are well distributed. Stir in the pumpkin puree, ensuring that the mixture is smooth before following it with the non-dairy milk and vanilla.

Meanwhile, heat a large, lightly greased skillet over medium heat on the stove.

Whisk the liquid mixture once more before using, and dip your first 4 pieces of toast (depending on how many will fit in your skillet), letting them soak for about 30 seconds before flipping and repeating. Once saturated, carefully lift the slices out with a large spatula and place them into the hot skillet. Fry for approximately 3–5 minutes per side, until browned and crisp on the outside, then transfer the toast to a plate, and repeat the process with the remaining bread. Serve with maple syrup, fruit spread, or powdered sugar as you see fit.

8 (1-Inch Thick) Slices Ciabatta or Baguette

2 Tablespoons Dark Brown Sugar, Firmly Packed

1 Teaspoon Instant Coffee Powder

1 Teaspoon Ground Cinnamon

¼ Teaspoon Ground Ginger

⅛ Teaspoon Ground Allspice

⅛ Teaspoon Ground Nutmeg

¼ Teaspoon Salt

½ Cup Pumpkin Puree

½ Cup Plain Nondairy Milk

1 Teaspoon Vanilla Extract

Red Velvet Smoothie

MAKES 1–2 SERVINGS

I can't lie: If there's leftover cake sitting out on the counter when I wake up, there's a good chance that I'll end up eating it for breakfast. Inevitably, the early AM sugar rush will send me spinning crazily through the day's tasks like an unbalanced top, yet I can never resist that sweet siren song. While blended beets will never rival the decadence of a tender-crumbed slice piled high with cream cheese frosting, this smoothie handily quashes red velvet cravings with fiber and protein to spare. Luscious ribbons of vanilla yogurt take the place of frosting, so the only thing you're really missing is the fork.

Toss the oats into your blender and pulse until broken down to a fine flour. Alternatively, feel free to start with previously ground oat flour to further expedite the process. Add in the flaxseeds, dates, beets, ice, and carrots, along with about ½ cup of the nondairy milk, and blend until smooth. Pour in the remainder of the milk, followed by the cocoa and cashew butter and vanilla extract, and thoroughly puree. If you don't have a high-speed blender, allow up to 5 minutes for the creamiest, silkiest consistency. Add in maple syrup according to taste if you prefer a sweeter smoothie.

Pour the smoothie into a tall glass. Add agave to the yogurt if your tastes skew on the sweeter side, and drizzle the mixture on top. Use your straw or a long spoon to swirl it in right before serving.

RED VELVET SMOOTHIE:

- ¼ Cup Old-Fashioned or Quick Cooking Rolled Oats
- 1 Tablespoon Ground Flaxseeds
- 4 Pitted Medjool Dates
- ⅔ Cup Diced Beets, Raw or Cooked
- ¼ Cup Ice Cubes
- ¼ Cup Diced or Shredded Carrots
- 1 Cup Unsweetened Nondairy Milk
- 2 Tablespoons Natural Cocoa Powder
- 1 Tablespoon Raw Cashew Butter
- ½ Teaspoon Vanilla Extract
- 1–2 Tablespoons 100% Grade B Maple Syrup (Optional)

YOGURT SWIRL:

- ⅓ Cup Vanilla Vegan Yogurt
- 1 Tablespoon Light Agave Nectar (Optional)

Stove Top Granola

When you barely have enough time to get dressed and wolf down breakfast in the morning, there certainly isn't time to stand around and wait for the oven to preheat. This mixture can easily be prepared ahead of time, ready when you are, but it comes together so quickly that you can start from scratch and still be done before the coffee has finished brewing. The combination of both old-fashioned and quick-cooking oats creates a satisfying matrix of sweet clusters, but you don't need to buy an entire container of both to make it happen. Lightly pulse ½ cup of whole rolled oats just until broken down to a very coarse meal, and you'll be good to go.

Begin by heating a large, dry skillet over medium heat and adding in both types of oats, nuts, and seeds. Stir frequently and cook just until toasted golden brown and highly aromatic, 1–3 minutes. Transfer to a large bowl and return the skillet to the stove.

Melt the coconut oil and mix in the maple syrup before introducing the ground flaxseeds, cinnamon, and salt. Stir well and let the mixture come to a lively bubble. Return the oat mixture to the pan, stirring vigorously to coat with the sticky mixture. Continue to cook, moving the granola around constantly to prevent it from burning, for about 5 minutes or so. Spread the mixture out on a baking sheet to allow it to cool quickly.

Sprinkle the dried fruits on top and stir them in. Serve as soon as you're hungry or let cool before digging in. Store in an airtight container at room temperature for up to 2 weeks. For even easier eating on the run, portion individual servings out into small ziplock bags and take your breakfast to go!

1½ Cups Old-Fashioned Rolled Oats

½ Cup Quick-Cooking Oats

¼ Cup Chopped Pecans or Walnuts

¼ Cup Pepitas or Sunflower Seeds

1 Tablespoon Coconut Oil

¼ Cup 100% Grade B Maple Syrup

3 Tablespoons Ground Flaxseeds

½ Teaspoon Ground Cinnamon

¼ Teaspoon Salt

¼ Cup Raisins

¼ Cup Dried Cranberries

Instantly transform this blend into a crunchy, healthy gingerbread treat by swapping the maple syrup for molasses, the dried cranberries for finely chopped crystalized ginger, and adding 1 teaspoon ground ginger.

Straight-Up Chickpea Scramble

MAKES 2 SERVINGS

Move over, tofu: There's a new bean in town shaking up the scramble scene. Chickpea flour rehydrates into creamy curds that are every bit as satisfying as eggs. Bulk up this foolproof base with as many vegetables as you can fit in your skillet, or keep things simple with just the essentials. It doesn't sound like much on its own, but the beauty of a good scramble is found in that very simplicity. Suitable for all moods and occasions, you can't go wrong by starting your day with a hearty, piping-hot portion.

Place a nonstick skillet over medium heat on the stove.

In a large bowl, whisk together the garbanzo bean flour, nutritional yeast, onion powder, smoked paprika, black salt, pepper, and turmeric. Make sure that all of the dry goods are equally distributed to ensure a smooth batter. Pour in the water and liquid aminos, stirring vigorously to beat out any lumps.

Melt the butter or coconut oil in the pan just before pouring in the chickpea mixture. Allow it to cook, undisturbed, for 1–2 minutes. It should begin to look dry around the edges when you can start scrambling. Use your spatula to break up the batter into curds as it thickens, continuing to stir until it forms more distinct clumps. Drizzle in the coconut milk, as needed, to keep things creamy and moist but not wet. When it's all said and done, the scramble should still be fairly soft and not browned.

Top with fresh chives or scallions, if desired, and serve right away.

- 1 Cup Garbanzo Bean Flour
- ¼ Cup Nutritional Yeast
- 1 Teaspoon Onion Powder
- ½ Teaspoon Smoked Paprika
- ½ Teaspoon Black Salt (Kala Namak)
- ¼ Teaspoon Ground Black Pepper
- ¼ Teaspoon Turmeric
- 1¼ Cups Vegetable Stock or Water
- 2 Teaspoons Bragg Liquid Aminos or Soy Sauce
- 2 Tablespoons Vegan Butter or Coconut Oil
- ⅓–⅔ Cup Full-Fat Coconut Milk
- Chives or Scallions, Thinly Sliced (Optional)

Sundae Smoothie Bowl

MAKES 1–2 SERVINGS

Acting like an adult can be a tough job, from making difficult decisions to working long hours, and dealing with all the monotony in between. It does, however, come with the side benefit that you have the authority to eat ice cream for breakfast whenever you want. In fact, it would be a very responsible and nutritious ruling to make every day a Sundae when the frosty treat in question is made of nothing but whole fruits and oats. If needed, bump it up to the next level with a scoop of plant-based protein powder, for those exceptionally strenuous days of adulting.

Chop the bananas into rough chunks and place them into your food processor along with the strawberries and oats. Pulse to break down the fruit, pausing to scrape down the sides of the bowl with your spatula as needed. Continue to blend while slowly streaming in the nondairy milk until smooth and creamy. Scoop or spoon into a bowl and stash it in the freezer while you prepare the chocolate sauce.

Simply whisk together the maple syrup, cocoa, and salt in a small bowl until smooth. Drizzle it generously over the bowl of ice cream, and top with whipped coconut cream, cherries, and/or nuts, to your heart's desire. Devour immediately!

SUNDAE SMOOTHIE BOWL:

- 2 Frozen Bananas
- ¾ Cup Sliced Strawberries
- ¼ Cup Rolled Quick-Cooking Oats
- 2–4 Tablespoons Vanilla Nondairy Milk

CHOCOLATE SAUCE:

- 2 Tablespoons 100% Grade B Maple Syrup
- 2 Tablespoons Dutch-Processed Cocoa Powder
- ⅛ Teaspoon Salt

ADDITIONAL TOPPINGS (OPTIONAL):

- Whipped Coconut Cream (page 26)
- Fresh Cherries
- Chopped Pecans, Walnuts, or Peanuts

Flavor variations are endless so don't be afraid to experiment. Swap out the strawberries for an additional frozen banana and add 2 tablespoons cocoa powder to make chocolate ice cream; 1 teaspoon of vanilla extract to make vanilla ice cream; ½ teaspoon peppermint extract and 2 tablespoons cacao nibs for mint chocolate chip ice cream. For a fruitier twist, trade the bananas for 1 cup frozen mango chunks or frozen sliced peaches.

Tofu Shakshuka

MAKES 2–4 SERVINGS

Though relatively unknown across the 50 united states, the word "shakshuka" is practically synonymous with breakfast in Israel. Young and old alike dig into bowls of this spicy red stew every morning, particularly relishing the poached eggs floating amongst the tomatoes and peppers. It's a simple pleasure that is just as easily translated for vegan tastes, complete with a punch of protein to start your day off right. Pair it with lightly toasted pita bread to serve more diners, or to satisfy for those with bigger appetites.

Start the stew simmering right away by tossing all the ingredients into a large pan set over medium heat on the stove. Add in the smaller amounts of crushed red pepper flakes and salt at the beginning, and adjust upward according to taste, if needed.

Meanwhile, toss the tofu into your food processor or blender along with the garbanzo bean flour, cornstarch, nutritional yeast, and black salt. Pulse to blend and incorporate all the ingredients, pausing to scrape down the sides of the bowl with a spatula as needed. Once the mixture is smooth, use a small cookie scoop to portion out 12 individual tofu balls and gently drop them into the bubbling red sauce. Simmer for 3–5 minutes, until cooked through. Garnish with minced parsley if desired and serve piping hot.

SHORTCUT SHAKSHUKA STEW:

1 Cup Roasted Red Peppers, Diced

2 Cups Marinara Sauce

1 Teaspoon Ground Cumin

½ Teaspoon Ground Coriander

½ Teaspoon Smoked Paprika

¼–½ Teaspoon Crushed Red Pepper Flakes

½–1 Teaspoon Salt

Minced Fresh Parsley (Optional)

POACHED TOFU:

8 Ounces (½ Package) Firm Tofu, Drained

½ Cup Garbanzo Bean Flour

2 Tablespoons Cornstarch

2 Tablespoons Nutritional Yeast

½ Teaspoon Black Salt (Kala Namak)

Quick Tip: Speed through the prep work by simply using plain cubed tofu or cooked chickpeas instead of making the dumpling-like poached tofu.

SNACKS AND APPS

All Dressed Potato Chip Nachos

MAKES 5–6 SERVINGS

Leave it to those imaginative Canadians to beat us at our own potato chip game. Once a rarity confined to the northern provinces, this cult classic has exploded on the scene and taken hold much like the equally decadent poutine. Barbecue sauce, sour cream, onion, ketchup, and vinegar may sound like a drunken kitchen experiment gone dreadfully awry, but something about the outrageous combination just hits all the right notes. These are usually potato chips already infused with this mélange of crave-worthy tastes thanks to the magic of modern food science, but my approach treats them more like nachos, piled high with said condiments and much fresher flavors. It may not be for everyone, but fans of the chip now have a whole new reason to get all dressed up for midnight snack.

Line a baking sheet with parchment paper or a silpat. Spread the chips out in an even layer and run them under the broiler, set to high, for 3–4 minutes. They should emerge warm and crispy; watch them carefully to make sure they don't burn.

Meanwhile, whisk together the barbecue sauce, sour cream or yogurt, and nutritional yeast.

Once satisfyingly toasted, drizzle the creamy barbecue sauce liberally over the chips, taking care to cover the potatoes evenly. There's nothing more disappointing than a dry chip in a sea of toppings. Even coverage is the key to achieving nacho greatness.

Sprinkle the diced tomato on top in the same fashion, followed by the red onion, sundried tomatoes, scallion, and dehydrated onion flakes, if using. Dig in immediately!

1 (5–6 Ounce) Bag Thick-Cut Salt and Vinegar Potato Chips

¼ Cup Barbecue Sauce*

2 Tablespoons Plain Vegan Sour Cream or Greek-Style Yogurt

1 Tablespoon Nutritional Yeast

1 Roma Tomato, Seeded and Diced

¼ Cup Thinly Sliced (About ¼ Medium) Red Onion

3 Tablespoons Julienned Sun-dried Tomatoes

1 Scallion, Sliced

1 Tablespoon Dehydrated Onion Flakes (Optional)

Don't buy, DIY! If you have an extra minute, whip up your own barbecue sauce from standard pantry staples. You'll be able to control the seasonings and sweetness, customizing the blend exactly as you want. Just whisk everything up and slather it on thick!

1 (5.5-Ounce) Can Tomato Paste
⅔ Cup Apple Cider Vinegar
¼ Cup 100% Grade B Maple Syrup
2 Tablespoons Molasses
2 Tablespoons Dijon Mustard

2 Tablespoons Garlic Powder
2 Tablespoons Smoked Paprika
1 Tablespoons Ground Black Pepper
1–2 Teaspoons Salt

SNACKS AND APPS 63

Buffalo Buttered Pecans

MAKES 1½ CUPS (ABOUT 6 SERVINGS)

Fusing the best of two popular bar bites into one addictive snack, these spicy pecans crackle with hot wing sauce while retaining a nutty, crisp crunch. Even if you're not much of a heat-seeker, the intensity and flavor is infinitely adjustable based on your hot sauce of choice. Frank's RedHot is most traditional, but I've had excellent results with standard issue sriracha and Tabasco as well. Don't be afraid to experiment, or scale back a bit for more timid palates. Great for gatherings big and small, you can just as easily double, triple, or quadruple the quantities to cover your entire crew.

Begin by melting the butter in a medium skillet and adding in the pecans. Cook for just a minute or two over medium heat to lightly toast the nuts, stirring and shaking the pan periodically. Once aromatic and gently browned, add in the hot sauce, sugar, vinegar, and garlic. Mix everything in and toss to coat.

Cook, stirring periodically over medium-high heat, for about 6–8 minutes, until the liquid has evaporated and the seasonings cling to the nuts. Sprinkle evenly with salt. Serve either warm or at room temperature.

The prepared pecans can be stored at room temperature in an airtight container for up to 1 week.

3 Tablespoons Vegan Butter

1½ Cups Raw Pecans

¼ Cup Hot Sauce

3 Tablespoons Granulated Sugar

2 Teaspoons Apple Cider Vinegar

1 Teaspoon Garlic Powder

½ Teaspoon Salt

Chili Relleno Rolls

MAKES 16–20 ROLLS AND 2½ CUPS DIPPING SAUCE; 8–10 SERVINGS

Stuffed to bursting, battered, and deep-fried, the typical chili relleno is basically a jalapeño popper on steroids. Roll up an instant fiesta by stripping away the greasy coating and replacing the stodgy fat bomb filling with a far more satisfying bean-based solution. Keeping a can or two of green chilies on hand means that these piquant bites are never more than a few minutes away, but fresh roasted peppers are always a welcome substitute. Bolder options include serranos or poblanos, whereas hatch or Anaheim might be more suitable for those with sensitive palates.

Start the dipping sauce first so it's ready to serve once you've got the chilies all rolled up. Puree the tomatoes, onion, and garlic in a blender until smooth. Heat the oil in a small saucepan over medium heat and add the tomato puree. Simmer for 5 minutes, stirring occasionally, until hot and slightly thickened but still somewhat brothy. Season with salt and pepper and keep warm.

Drain and rinse the chilies before slicing them in half. Set aside on a paper towel to let them dry out a bit.

Prepare the cheesy filling by roughly mashing the beans into a chunky paste. You can do this by hand with a sturdy potato masher or by pulsing the beans briefly in your food processor or blender. Add in the nutritional yeast, yogurt, tahini, vinegar, garlic powder, onion powder, paprika, pepper, and salt, mashing vigorously to incorporate. Finally, fold in the panko to help thicken the mixture.

Spoon about a tablespoon or so into the center of each chili strip. Wrap the chili around the cheesy bean mix, securing with a toothpick. Repeat until all the chilies are filled. Serve at room temperature or warm gently in the oven at 350°F for about 5 minutes.

Quick Fix: Blend 2½ cups of prepared salsa into a smooth puree instead of cooking up the dipping sauce from scratch.

FRESH TOMATO DIPPING SAUCE:

5 Medium Tomatoes, Diced (About 2½ Cups)

½ Medium Yellow Onion, Diced (About ½ Cup)

1 Clove Garlic, Minced

1 Tablespoon Olive Oil

½ Teaspoon Salt

¼ Teaspoon Ground Black Pepper

CHILI RELLENO ROLLS:

2 (7-Ounce) Cans Whole Roasted Green Chilies

1 (14-Ounce) Can (1½ Cups Cooked) Navy Beans, Rinsed and Thoroughly Drained

¼ Cup Nutritional Yeast

¼ Cup Plain, Unsweetened Vegan Yogurt

2 Tablespoons Tahini

1 Tablespoon Apple Cider Vinegar

1 Teaspoon Garlic Powder

½ Teaspoon Onion Powder

½ Teaspoon Smoked Paprika

¼ Teaspoon Cayenne Pepper

¼ Teaspoon Salt

⅓ Cup Panko Bread Crumbs

Hurricane Popcorn

MAKES APPROXIMATELY 4 QUARTS; 4–6 SERVINGS

Visiting Hawaii for the first time, there were only a few foods I knew were must-eats, and hurricane popcorn was near the top. A simple concept that has won fiercely loyal fans, boxes are said to be smuggled back the mainland by those in the know, craving the distinctive island snack food. Microwave bags burst with hot butter-flavored oil, fluffy kernels glistening with the with artificial umami elixir, utterly irresistible but admittedly unsavory when it comes down to bare ingredients. In the same vein as "slimy yet satisfying," that addictive snack made a lasting impression as "good but greasy." Certainly, we can all do better . . . And after returning home, that's exactly what I did.

In a large stock pot with high sides, heat the coconut oil over medium-high heat. Place 3–4 popcorn kernels in the pot, cover, and once one pops, that will mean your oil has come up to the right temperature to really get popping. Add the remaining unpopped popcorn into the pan and cover the pan once more.

Gently shake the pan over the heat, still covered, to pop the kernels evenly and prevent already popped corn from burning. When the pace of popping slows to one pop every 3–5 seconds, remove the pan from the heat. Keep the pot covered while the final kernels pop, about 3 minutes. Carefully lift the lid away from you, as there will be a good deal of very hot steam looking to escape.

Meanwhile, melt the butter in a microwave-safe dish, heating for 30–60 seconds. Transfer the popped corn to your desired serving bowl, leaving any unpopped kernels in the bottom of the pot. Drizzle the melted butter all over, tossing to coat. Sprinkle in the nori flakes, sesame seeds, and salt, to taste. Finally add the rice crackers right on top, and stir gently to incorporate. Enjoy right away!

- 2 Tablespoons Coconut Oil
- ½ Cup Popcorn Kernels
- 3 Tablespoons Vegan Butter
- 3–4 Tablespoons Powdered, Flaked, or Shredded Nori
- 2 Tablespoons Toasted Sesame Seeds
- ¼–½ Teaspoon Salt
- 1 Cup Japanese Rice Crackers

Lighten up by cutting back on the oil and air-popping your corn in the microwave. Place the uncooked kernels in a paper bag and fold closed, securing the flap with a strip of tape. Microwave for 2½–3 minutes at full power, until the popping sounds slow to about 2 seconds between pops. Let the bag rest for 30 seconds before opening, and be careful to avoid the hot steam when breaking the seal. Omit the coconut oil entirely and cut the melted vegan butter down to 1 tablespoon.

Island Breeze Ceviche

MAKES 4–6 SERVINGS

Contrary to popular belief, ceviche needn't include any seafood to be considered "authentic," or more importantly, to be considered delicious. One of many dishes with murky origins, it's largely credited to the Peruvians, but it made its mark on cultures across all continents. If one were to look at the Latin etymology, it would simply mean "food for men and animals," a murky free-for-all with very little meaning other than the fact that it was, indeed, edible. Turning to Arabic, we see the foundation for "cooking in vinegar." Persian linguists would agree, going further to suggest that it was a "vinegar soup." Sure, fish or meat was almost always invited to the party, but that doesn't mean it was essential to the soul of the dish.

Scores of creative ceviches abound, but the most successful ones take texture into account before flavor, counterintuitive as that may sound. So much of the overall eating experience relies on texture, which is why fresh, juicy lychee became the basis for this plant-based rendition. Somewhat meaty yet springy much like shrimp or calamari, it's an improbable but highly successful seafood substitute.

Want to mix it up? Consider ripe tomatoes, marinated mushrooms, chunks of fried plantain, or steamed sweet potatoes, just for starters. Borrow from as many different cultures as you like; for ceviche, as long as it's cold and raw, pretty much anything goes. The only inviolable rule is to use ONLY fresh lychees. If you can't find fresh, just double up on the coconut, and choose your own vegetable adventure from there.

To prepare ceviche, simply toss everything together in a large bowl except for the salt, cover, and let marinate for as long as you can bear to wait, but at least 5 minutes to allow the flavors to mingle and meld. Season with salt to taste and serve thoroughly chilled, with crackers if desired.

10–12 Fresh Lychees, Peeled, Pitted, and Quartered (About ⅔ Cup)

1 Fresh Young Thai Coconut, Meat Removed and Diced

½ Large Cucumber, Peeled and Seeded

1 Small Avocado, Diced

3 Tablespoons Lime Juice

1 Tablespoon Pineapple Juice

1 Tablespoon Rice Vinegar

1 tablespoon Vegan Fish Sauce or Soy Sauce

1 Red Jalapeno, Seeded and Finely Minced

2 Scallions, Thinly Sliced

¼ Cup Packed Fresh Cilantro, Roughly Chopped

Salt, to Taste

Pesto Tomato Poppers

MAKES 10–16 SERVINGS

Tender leaves of fresh basil, still radiating heat from the sun's gentle caress, are the purest manifestation of summer in edible format. Plucked straight off the vine at the peak of perfection, the intensity of their herbaceous flavor practically vibrates with life, an infectious energy that you can't help but smile about. Even if they were to overrun every square inch of my garden, I'd still never be able to get enough, mowing down fields of the stuff in a minute through the magic of pesto. This herb-powered sauce goes well with almost anything you can think of, but of course has a special affinity for its next-door seasonal neighbors, tomatoes and avocados. Dainty cherry tomatoes provide a more socially appropriate vehicle for consuming untold quantities of pesto in public, much to the delight of fellow basil-lovers abroad. The very same concept could be effortlessly converted into a winning side dish by hollowing out and stuffing larger, sturdy tomatoes instead.

Toss the basil, garlic, 2 tablespoons of the pine nuts, salt, and pepper into your food processor. Pulse to begin breaking down the nuts and leaves, pausing to scrape down the sides of the bowl to ensure that everything gets incorporated. Keep the mixture somewhat rough; you're not trying to make a puree here. Scoop out the flesh of the avocado and add it along with the red wine vinegar. Pulse to incorporate, until creamy but still slightly chunky.

Slice off the top ¼ of each tomato. Use a small spoon or melon baller to scoop out the watery seeds inside, and either discard or save for another recipe (they're great for cooking down into soup or pasta sauce!).

Spoon a generous measure of the pesto mixture into the tomatoes and top with the remaining pine nuts. Serve immediately.

- 1 Large Bunch (Approximately 2 Cups) Fresh Basil Leaves
- 2 Cloves Garlic, Minced
- 3 Tablespoons Toasted Pine Nuts, Divided
- ½ Teaspoon Salt
- ¼ Teaspoon Freshly Ground Black Pepper
- 1 Medium, Ripe Avocado
- 1½ Tablespoons Red Wine Vinegar
- 1 Pound Large Cherry or Grape Tomatoes

Quick Fix: In a rush? Skip the stuffing; dice the avocado, halve the tomatoes, and simply toss everything with the pesto mixture. Serve as a salad and call it a day.

Helpful Hint: If your tomatoes are on a roll, line your serving plate with frilly lettuce to help keep them upright.

Pizza Hummus

It's a long-standing joke that if I favor some sort of store-bought comestible, and especially if I'm head-over-heels in love with it, then that's pretty much the kiss of death for that particular product. Thus, my saga of The Pizza Hummus should shock exactly no one. I was madly in love, head over heels, after the very first package, but that one package was all that I ever got. Weeks passed. Months crept by. The hummus never even showed up at the grocery store again, and I never heard another peep about it, like a bad boyfriend who "forgot" to call.

Finally growing frustrated at this unrequited longing, I took matters into my own hands and came up with an even more passionate affair. Saturated with umami flavor, it's like a roasted tomato puree, voluptuous "cheese" sauce, and the creamiest hummus possible all wrapped up in one spreadable, dippable package. Just a touch of red pepper flakes lend a faint, piquant bite, exactly the way a good slice ought to. The only thing missing is perhaps a paper-thin, crunchy crust, but just stock up on your favorite crackers, and it's a done deal.

Place the sun-dried tomatoes into your food processor or blender. Add in the roasted garlic, and pulse briefly just to break down the two to a coarse pulp and make them easier to incorporate later. Follow that with all the other ingredients, and make sure you start with just ¼ teaspoon of salt now so that you can adjust it to taste later. Let the motor run until everything is mostly combined; it will probably look fairly dry. Stop, scrape down the sides of the bowl, and then with the motor running, begin to stream in the leftover oil that was packed with the sun-dried tomatoes, until it reaches a consistency you're happy with. For a lighter option, simply use water instead. Taste, add more salt if needed, and then let the machine run for another 5–10 minutes, until the hummus is velvety smooth and creamy.

To serve, try topping it with your favorite pizza add-ons, such as finely chopped vegan pepperoni, sliced olives, roasted red peppers, sautéed mushrooms, or anything else you like on your pie!

½ Cup Oil-Packed Sun-Dried Tomatoes, Drained and Roughly Chopped

3 Cloves Roasted or 1 Clove Raw Garlic

1 15-Ounce Can Chickpeas, Rinsed and Drained

3 Tablespoons Lemon Juice

⅓ Cup Nutritional Yeast

2 Tablespoons Olive Oil, Plus More for Garnish (Optional)

2 Tablespoons Fresh Parsley

1 Tablespoon Fresh Basil

½ Teaspoon Dried Oregano

1 Tablespoon Barley Miso Paste

½ Teaspoon Ground Cumin

Pinch Red Pepper Flakes

¼–¾ Teaspoon Salt

Puppermint Patties

MAKES 10–16 PATTIES

If you can take 10 minutes to feed yourself and your loved ones, why can't you do the same to make something special for your four-legged friends too? Granted, my go-to treats are simply raw carrots, which take no prep work at all, but it's nice to get some variety for the sake of nutrition—and of course, fun! Chocolate is dangerous for dogs, which is why carob handily carries the torch here for this minty biscuit. Using fresh herbs has the side benefit of freshening breath, so everyone can appreciate your extra effort. Even the pickiest eaters will be begging for seconds.

Place the coconut and oats in your food processor and pulse until ground to a coarse flour. Add in the mint, carob powder, and chia seeds, and pulse for another minute or two to break down the leaves and incorporate all the other ingredients. With the motor running, slowly drizzle in both the melted coconut oil and nondairy milk. Pause to scrape down the sides of the bowl as needed, until the mixture forms into a cohesive dough.

Scoop out small balls about the size of walnuts and flatten them lightly with the palms of your hands. Chill in the fridge to further set the patties, or serve right away. Store in the fridge in an airtight container for up to a week, or in the freezer for up to three months.

1 Cup Shredded, Unsweetened Coconut

⅓ Cup Old-Fashioned Rolled Oats

⅓ Cup Fresh Mint, Roughly Chopped

2 Tablespoons Carob Powder

1 Tablespoon Chia Seeds

¼ Cup Coconut Oil, Melted

1–2 Tablespoons Plain Nondairy Milk

Quick Tip: To make these treats tastier for humans, sweeten the deal by adding ½ cup confectioner's sugar.

Summer Corn Queso

MAKES ABOUT 2 CUPS; 4–6 SERVINGS

There are few things that can't be improved by a good queso sauce. Boring pizza? Lavish it with creamy queso. Dry tacos? Ladle that queso right on in. Bland baked potato? Stodgy sandwich? Lackluster soup? Okay, I think you know where this is going. My point is that this stuff is as good as liquid gold, and having the right dairy-free queso in your culinary toolbelt is the answer to pretty much anything, no matter the question. Start with whole vegetables and half the work is already done for you. Fresh sweet corn really makes this queso sing, but frozen also works beautifully when it's not in season. The only trouble is that you'll keep thinking of new dishes to use it on, but it's so tempting unadorned, it's tough to do much more than serve it up with crunchy chips and call it a day.

Place the oil in a medium saucepan set over medium heat. Add in the corn kernels and garlic, sautéing until lightly toasted and golden brown all over, about 4 minutes. Meanwhile, whisk together the nondairy milk, nutritional yeast, miso paste, cornstarch, paprika, cumin, salt, and red pepper flakes, beating vigorously to prevent any lumps from forming.

Pour the liquid into the hot pan and bring up to a full boil. The mixture should thicken considerably in that time. Transfer half to your blender to keep the finished queso on the chunkier side, ideal for dipping, or add it all in if you'd prefer a completely smooth sauce. Puree until silky smooth, pausing to scrape down the sides of the blender if needed. Stir the puree in with the remainder if you opted to separate the mix, top with scallions, and serve warm.

¼ Cup Olive Oil

2 Cups Fresh or Frozen and Thawed Corn Kernels

1 Clove Garlic, Finely Minced

1 Cup Plain, Unsweetened Nondairy Milk

3 Tablespoons Nutritional Yeast

1 Tablespoon White Miso Paste

2 Teaspoon Cornstarch

¾ Teaspoon Smoked Paprika

½ Teaspoon Ground Cumin

½ Teaspoon Salt

¼–½ Teaspoon Crushed Red Pepper Flakes

2 Scallions, Thinly Sliced

Quick Tip: You can sometimes find fire-roasted corn in the freezer section, which will infuse instant smoky, roasted flavor and reduce the overall cooking time significantly.

Tempeh Fries

MAKES 2–4 SERVINGS

Chickens don't have fingers and fish aren't shaped like sticks, so while this tantalizing tempeh dipper isn't a French fry in the traditional sense, I don't feel any compunction about labeling it as such. Crispy on the outside and bursting with hearty protein on the inside, they'd beat out most limp potato variations anyhow, no matter what you call them. Better yet, there's no need to haul out a giant vat of oil for deep frying, since these killer apps are cooked over the stove top. Creamy peanut satay sauce is the sidekick to this new snack time superhero, but it's no meek bit player here. I've been known to make double, triple, and quadruple batches to have extra for slathering over salads and pasta dishes for days to come.

Place a large skillet over high heat and allow it to get blazing hot. In a large bowl, whisk both oils, soy sauce, paprika, and coriander together. Add in the tempeh strips, tossing them gently to coat. Pour the mixture, excess marinade and all, into the pan. Stand back slightly and prepare yourself for the sizzle! Turn the heat down slightly to medium-high, and spread the tempeh out in an even layer, making sure that each piece has full contact with the bottom of the pan. You want to fry them, after all, not steam them.

Meanwhile, simply whisk together all the ingredients for the peanut satay sauce so that it's ready when you are. If you really want to power through this step, just toss everything into your blender or food processor and let it go to town. Transfer the mixture to a small saucepan and gently warm it over medium-low heat. Bring it just to the brink of boiling, at which point it should have thickened nicely. It will continue to thicken as it cools, so you may want to add water to reach your desired consistency, or if you prepare it in advance.

After about 3–4 minutes, the tempeh should be nicely browned on the bottom. Flip it over and repeat with the opposite side. When crisp and brown all over, your fries are ready to serve! Plate them with a dish of peanut satay sauce on the side.

TEMPEH FRIES:

- 1 Tablespoon Olive Oil
- 1 Tablespoon Toasted Sesame Oil
- 1½ Tablespoons Soy Sauce
- ½ Teaspoon Hot Paprika
- ½ Teaspoon Ground Coriander
- 8 Ounces Tempeh, Sliced Crosswise into ½-Inch Strips

PEANUT SATAY SAUCE:

- ¼ Cup Full-Fat Coconut Milk
- ¼ Cup Creamy Peanut Butter
- 2 Tablespoons Lime Juice
- 2 Teaspoons Soy Sauce
- 1 Teaspoon Light Agave Nectar
- ½ Teaspoon Ground Ginger
- ¼ Teaspoon Garlic Powder
- ¼–½ Teaspoon Sriracha
- ¼ Teaspoon Ground Coriander
- ¼ Teaspoon Salt

Teriyaki Edamame

MAKES 4–6 SERVINGS

Teriyaki, that sticky amber lacquer found glazing all manner of grilled foods with equal finesse, lends its universal charm to the humble podded soybean. Quickly charred in a hot pan, the edamame take on a lustrous sheen as they sizzle and simmer in the sauce. Granted, it's something of a messy snack to behold, but you could spin the situation as a positive, because it's just finger-licking good.

Heat the sesame oil in a large skillet over high heat, adding in the minced garlic, ginger, and edamame as soon as it begins to shimmer. Sauté for 2–3 minutes until aromatic and lightly browned. Pour in the soy sauce and pineapple juice, mix thoroughly to combine, and let the mixture cook for 4 minutes.

Meanwhile, whisk together the vinegar, brown sugar, and cornstarch, ensuring that there are no clumps of starch remaining before pouring everything into the skillet. Continue to cook for another 2–3 minutes until the mixture is thick and syrupy, thoroughly coating the edamame. Sprinkle with sesame seeds and serve immediately.

2 Tablespoons Toasted Sesame Oil

2 Cloves Garlic, Minced

1 Teaspoon Minced Fresh Ginger

1 Pound Frozen Edamame, in the Pod

¼ Cup Soy Sauce

¼ Cup Pineapple Juice

2 Tablespoons Rice Vinegar

2 Tablespoons Dark Brown Sugar, Firmly Packed

2 Teaspoons Cornstarch

2 Teaspoons Sesame Seeds

Quick Tip: Hungry guests arrive unannounced, in need of nourishment ASAP? Get this snack on the table in half the time sautéing 1 pound of edamame with ½–⅔ cup of prepared teriyaki sauce instead. Bump up the flavor with ground ginger and powdered garlic, to taste.

Wasabi Pea Fritters

MAKES 10–12 FRITTERS

Wasabi peas used to be a terribly exotic snack. My friends and I would trek many miles to tiny Japanese markets hidden within the city, well before the days of online shopping, just to score a handful of these blazing hot morsels. The best ones would hit you right in the sinuses and make your eyes water immediately, so pungent and powerful that our meager stock could still last for weeks. Increased accessibility still hasn't damped my enthusiasm for that addictive amalgamation, although the unrestrained blast of heat doesn't quite do the trick anymore. Applying wasabi paste with greater finesse in the kitchen, pea fritters offer both a fresher and more vibrant solution to those familiar cravings. If you want even crispier results, try frying spoonfuls of batter in 1–2 inches of neutral oil at 365°F for 3–5 minutes, until they float.

Begin heating the oil in a large skillet over medium heat.

Meanwhile, toss the peas into your food processor along with the wasabi paste, vinegar, garlic, and aquafaba. Pulse until you achieve a chunky sort of mash, scraping down the sides of the bowl as needed. Add in the flour, baking powder, and ½ teaspoon of the salt, pulsing again to incorporate.

Line a wire rack with paper towels in preparation for the finished fritters. Turning your attention to the hot oil, use a medium ice cream or cookie scoop to dole out mounds of approximately 3 tablespoons of batter per fritter. Cook the fritters for 2 to 3 minutes on each side, flipping when golden brown. Transfer the fritters to the wire rack to sop up any excess oil, season with the reserved salt, and repeat the cooking process with the remaining batter. Serve hot, literally.

2 Tablespoons Olive Oil

2 Cups Frozen Peas, Thawed

1½–2 Tablespoons Wasabi Paste

1 Tablespoon Rice Vinegar

1 Teaspoon Garlic Powder

½ Cup Aquafaba

¾ Cup All-Purpose Flour

¾ Teaspoon Baking Powder

¾ Teaspoon Salt, Divided

Though the bold taste of these fritters really speaks for itself, pairing a creamy, cooling dip is never a bad idea. My go-to blend is made of ¾ cup unsweetened, plain vegan yogurt, 1 tablespoon rice vinegar, 1 finely shredded Persian cucumber, 1 teaspoon garlic powder, and salt and pepper to taste. Use vegan mayonnaise or sour cream instead of yogurt for a richer experience.

SALADS

Broccoli Crunch Salad

MAKES 4–6 SERVINGS

Raw broccoli may sound more like a kid's worst nightmare than tasty picnic fare, but hear me out on this one. Impeccably fresh florets have a crisp texture and verdant green flavor that is lost the moment they mingle with heat. Satisfying with a hearty crunch, even when dressed well in advance, it's no struggle to mow down a whole head of the stuff when it's bathed in cooling yet tangy ranch dressing. Layering it in glass jars makes for an impressive presentation when taking it on the go, but such formalities needn't slow you down. Just toss everything together and pack it away for later; every bite will be just as fresh and vibrant for brunch, lunch, or dinner later on.

Since the salad itself comes together so quickly and effortlessly, prepare the dressing first. Simply whisk together all the ingredients in a large bowl until completely smooth. Voilà, it's ready to use! You may have more than you need to for this recipe, but it keeps very well in an airtight container in the fridge, for 1–2 weeks.

If you'd like to make the layered version of this recipe, start by spooning about ¼–⅓ cup of dressing into the bottoms of 4–6 glass mason jars. Equally distribute the vegetables, fruits, and nuts in the order listed between the jars, evenly spreading them across each fresh layer. Seal and keep refrigerated until ready to serve. When you want to enjoy, shake it up to coat all the goodies with dressing and dig in! Simplify the mix by just tossing everything together and serving immediately.

*Still can't stomach completely raw broccoli? I feel your pain. Quickly blanch florets by tossing them in boiling water or microwaving for 2 minutes. Immediately plunge into ice water to stop the cooking process and retain a bright green color. Alternatively, consider using broccoli raab (otherwise known as rapini) instead, which is naturally more tender and mild.

YOGURT RANCH DRESSING:

- ¾ Cup Plain, Unsweetened Vegan Yogurt
- 1 Tablespoon Lemon Juice
- 2 Tablespoons Apple Cider Vinegar
- 2 Tablespoons Olive Oil
- 1½ Teaspoons Light Agave Nectar
- 1½ Teaspoons Onion Powder
- ½ Teaspoon Garlic Powder
- ½ Teaspoon Dried Dill Weed
- ½ Teaspoon Salt

BROCCOLI SALAD:

- 4 Cups (About 2 Medium Crowns) Broccoli Florets, Raw or Lightly Blanched*
- 1 Cup Shredded Carrots
- 1 Sweet Red Apple, Cored, Quartered, and Thinly Sliced
- ½ Medium Red Onion, Quartered and Thinly Sliced
- ½ Cup Toasted Whole Cashews

Citrus Carpaccio

MAKES 2–3 SERVINGS

Paper-thin slices of meat are typically the calling card of traditional carpaccio preparations, but my take is a tribute to the bounty of winter produce. It's a drastic stretch of the definition, perhaps, but I promise that no one will ask "Where's the beef?" when this dazzling platter hits the table. As bold in flavor as it is in color and texture, sweet and tart citrus meet crisp, peppery radishes and greens, accented by whispers of licorice-scented fennel. Impossibly complex for such a simple concept, it feels almost silly to write out a full recipe for instructions, yet to withhold such a brilliant formula would seem a crime. Dazzling fresh fruits and vegetables are essential as one might imagine, but the most important ingredient is one that you won't actually taste: a sharp knife. Hone your blade and your skills to make quick, clean work of this dish.

Slice off the peels from all the citrus and cut them crosswise, about 2 or 3 millimeters in thickness. Pop out any seeds you might encounter and discard. Peel the beet and slice as thinly as possible, along with the radish, daikon, and fennel, between 1–2 millimeters, ideally. Either toss everything together in a large bowl or arrange attractively on a large platter, depending on how fancy you want to get. Top with watercress, pistachios, and a drizzle of oil. Finish by sprinkling evenly with salt right before serving.

- 1 Pink Grapefruit
- 1 White Grapefruit
- 1 Blood Orange
- 1 Gold Beet
- 1 Red Radish
- 1 Purple or Small White Daikon
- ½ Bulb Fennel, Fronds Removed
- 1 Cup Watercress
- ¼ Cup Toasted Pistachios, Coarsely Chopped
- 2 Tablespoons Olive Oil
- ¼ Teaspoon Salt

Quick Tip: Use a mandoline to power through those fruits and vegetables at warp speed, with greater consistency possible than with manual slicing. Just use a slightly larger allowance for the citrus than the hard vegetables, since they're liable to simply turn into juice at a finer grade.

Everything Bagel Salad

MAKES 2–4 SERVINGS

Brunch in old-school Brooklyn meant one thing and one thing only: a fresh, untoasted everything bagel slathered with cream cheese and piled high with slivers of cured or smoked salmon. Slices of tomatoes, red onions, and capers are all permissible additions, and you can probably sneak in a few rounds of cucumber or tendrils of fresh dill to really gild the lily, but all other intrusions will only draw the ire and scorn of natives in the know. No doubt, this avant-garde spin would be an affront to native New Yorkers, suggesting that the crowning jewel of the whole assembly could be made of carrots rather than seafood— and that doesn't even touch on the whole lettuce controversy.

I could never claim to have perfected the art form nor improved upon the classic, but I will say that these flavors resonate in just the same way, satisfying a long unfulfilled craving like nothing else. Carrot strips make an unlikely stand-in for fish, but their natural sweetness mingles with the smoky essence in a way that leaves even pescatarians impressed. All you really need is a heaping stack of it on top of the standard sandwich to craft the best brunch in any town. Spreading out the "lox" love in a leafy salad is an extra-special treat for a weekend or weekday indulgence.

To make the "lox," use your vegetable peeler to shave the carrots into paper-thin ribbons. Place them in a microwave-safe bowl along with the liquid aminos or soy sauce, oil, and liquid smoke. Toss to combine and heat on full power for 1 minute. Stir thoroughly and heat for another minute. Let sit for a minute and toss the mixture in the fridge to cool it down quickly.

Meanwhile, prepare the dressing by simply mixing together all of the ingredients until smooth and creamy. If the cream cheese is cold, you may need to use some real elbow grease to break it down properly. Incorporate the liquid ingredients a little bit at a time, whisking vigorously as you go. Drizzle in additional water if needed to reach a pourable consistency.

Finally, assembling the salad is a snap. Toss together the lettuce, cucumber, tomato, onion, and capers (if using) and drizzle in enough dressing to coat but not soak the vegetables. Transfer to a large bowl or serving platter and top with bagel chips and strands of carrot lox. Serve right away.

CARROT LOX:

- 2 Large Carrots (About 4–5 Ounces Each), Peeled
- 1½ Tablespoons Bragg Liquid Aminos or Soy Sauce
- 1 Tablespoon Olive Oil
- 1 Teaspoons Liquid Smoke

CREAM CHEESE BAGEL DRESSING:

- ½ Cup Vegan Cream Cheese
- 2 Tablespoons Lemon Juice
- 1 Tablespoon Olive Oil
- 1 Tablespoon Dehydrated Onion Flakes
- 1 Teaspoon Garlic Powder
- 1 Teaspoon Toasted Sesame Seeds
- ½ Teaspoon Poppy Seeds
- ½ Teaspoon Dijon Mustard

Continued on page 94

* If you're a master multi-tasker, you can even bust out home-made bagel chips from scratch in no time at all. The bulk of that time is inactive while the bread bakes, so start it cooking right away to maximize your time in the kitchen. The thinner you slice your bagel, the crispier the chips, and the faster they'll cook, too.

Preheat your oven or toaster oven to 350°F.

Toss the bagel slices with the olive oil until evenly coated, and spread them out in a single layer on baking sheet lined with parchment paper or a silpat. Bake for 8–10 minutes, until golden brown and crisp. Flip about halfway through the baking process if the bagel pieces aren't all browning at an equal rate.

Cool before using or store in an airtight container for up to 2 weeks.

¼ Teaspoon Salt

⅛ Teaspoon Ground Black Pepper

Salad:

1 Head Romaine Lettuce, Chopped (About 5–6 Cups)

1 Small Seedless Cucumber, Sliced (About 1 Cup)

2 Large Tomatoes, Sliced (About 1 Cup)

¼ Small Red Onion, Thinly Sliced (About ⅓ Cup)

1–2 Tablespoons Capers, Drained (Optional)

½ Cup Everything Bagel Chips, Store-Bought or Homemade*

Basic Bagel Chips:

1 (4-Ounce) Everything Bagel, Sliced into ⅛- to ¼-Inch Rounds

1 Tablespoon Olive Oil

Grilled Caesar Salad

MAKES 2–4 SERVINGS

Applying heat to lettuce goes against everything I've been taught about the proper treatment of delicate leafy greens. Scared off by visions of slimy, wilted iceberg, the mere concept of tossing a few defenseless heads of romaine onto a roaring grill sounds like some nauseating joke. Heat and its transformative properties have the last laugh though; screaming hot grates merely char the surface, imparting a bold new world of flavor in their wake while leaving the refreshingly crisp core intact. Caesar salad, with its elegant simplicity and briny, umami dressing is an ideal canvas. Serve it as a side dish or bulk it up with rich chunks of avocado and cubes of smoked tofu to convert it into a show-stopping main course.

Fire up your grill or stovetop grill pan over high heat. Prepare the croutons by brushing the slices of bread with oil and sprinkle evenly with salt. Toss the pieces on the grill, turning once, and cook until golden and crisp. Transfer to a cutting board and dice into rough cubes.

Meanwhile, toss all the ingredients for the dressing into your blender except for the water. Thoroughly puree, scraping down the sides of the container as needed to get everything incorporated, until completely smooth. Slowly drizzle in the water with the motor running, until it reaches your desired consistency.

GRILLED CROUTONS:
- **2–3 1-Inch Thick Slices (2.5 Ounces) Ciabatta or Baguette**
- **1 Tablespoon Olive Oil**
- **¼ Teaspoon Salt**

Continued on page 97

Slice the romaine hearts in half lengthwise, brush evenly with oil and then grill with cut sides down. The cooking surface must be absolutely screaming hot so that the lettuce needs only a minute or two to take on dark grill marks.

To serve, either plate the romaine whole and sprinkle with croutons, capers, hemp seeds (if using), and dressing to taste, or cut the romaine into bite-sized pieces and simply toss everything together in a large bowl. Serve immediately.

CAESAR DRESSING:

½ Cup Cooked White Beans

2 Tablespoons Tahini

1 Tablespoon White Miso Paste

1 Tablespoon Nutritional Yeast

1 Teaspoon Capers, Thoroughly Drained

1 Clove Garlic, Chopped

2 Tablespoons Lemon Juice

¼ Teaspoon Ground Black Pepper

¼ Cup Olive Oil

2–4 Tablespoons Water

SALAD AND ASSEMBLY:

3 Hearts (About 1½ Pounds) Romaine Lettuce

1 Tablespoon Olive Oil

2 Teaspoons Capers, Thoroughly Drained

1 Tablespoon Hemp Seeds (Optional)

Quick Tip: Swap out the grilled croutons for your favorite prepared variety or go gluten-free by using crispy seasoned chickpeas instead.

Snack attack? Omit the water from the dressing and use it as a dip with raw vegetables, chips, or crackers.

Falafel Fattoush

MAKES 4–6 SERVINGS

If you took falafel but skipped all the mashing, mixing, and deep frying, you'd get the gist of this herbaceous Middle Eastern panzanella, also known as a bread salad. Deconstructed dishes get a bad rap in this postmodern culinary scene, but just this once, I wouldn't take offense at the term. Everything you'd want from a good falafel sandwich can be found in this abundant bowl, simply chopped and tossed for a fresher, more flavorful experience with every forkful. The pita become soggy fairly quickly, so don't delay after tossing it with the dressing: Dig right in immediately, or withhold the olive oil and lemon juice until you're ready to serve.

Lightly toast the pita bread and chop it into bite-sized squares, about ½-inch each. Place the bread in a large bowl along with the tomatoes, cucumber, chickpeas, scallions, and parsley. Mix the vegetables around lightly to combine. Sprinkle in the minced garlic, red pepper flakes, cumin, coriander, ½ teaspoon salt, and pepper. Toss everything together until the vegetables are well distributed and evenly coated with the spices.

Right before serving, drizzle in the lemon juice and olive oil, tossing once more to incorporate. Add more salt to taste, if needed, and finish with a sprinkle of sesame seeds over the top.

4 (2-Ounce) Pita Breads

1 Pint Cherry Tomatoes (Halved if Large)

1 Cup Sliced Persian Cucumber or Diced English Cucumber

1 15-Ounce Can Chickpeas, Rinsed and Drained

2 Scallions, Thinly Sliced

1 Cup Fresh Parsley Leaves

1 Clove Garlic, Finely Minced

¼–½ Teaspoon Crushed Red Pepper Flakes

2 Teaspoons Ground Cumin

2 Teaspoons Ground Coriander

½–1 Teaspoon Salt

⅛ Teaspoon Ground Black Pepper

1 Tablespoon Lemon Juice

2 Tablespoons Olive Oil

2 Tablespoons Sesame Seeds, Toasted

Guavacado Chopped Salad

MAKES 4–6 SERVINGS

Over three million tons of guava are produced in India alone, and yet the tropical fruit is relatively unknown in North America. Such a shame to never know the charms of its tangy, sour flesh, the acidic antidote to many syrupy-sweet fruit salads. Worse yet is the lack of interest in exploring less traveled paths, weaving the so-called "sand plum" into more savory adventures. Apple guavas are among the most popular varieties, and the one you'll want to seek out for this invigorating raw preparation. Colored like a green apple, with similarly tart flavor to match, slice one open to release a fragrant bouquet of exotic aromatics, singing with the bright zeal of citrus and mysterious floral redolence. Each fruit is unique, some with more notes of pineapple, papaya, banana, and lemon, but when tossed together make a winsome chopped salad. You really can't go wrong when everyday luxuries like avocados, papayas, and macadamia nuts get involved, so if you've never tried guava before, consider this an ideal introduction, and chop to it!

As for any good chopped salad, make sure all the fruits and vegetables are cut into approximately equal pieces. From there, you can pretty much make this recipe with your eyes closed. Simply toss everything together in a large bowl, coating all the ingredients evenly and making sure all components are equally distributed throughout.

If you'd like to really break things down like serious chopped salad institutions do, lay all the greens and fruits out on a large cutting board and continuously run your knife through the whole pile, going back and forth in different directions, until the mixture reaches your desired consistency. From there, add in the water chestnuts, macadamia nuts, lime juice, oil, salt, and pepper. Toss as before, transfer to a large bowl, and serve right away.

2 Cups Romaine or Butter Lettuce, Roughly Chopped

2 Cups Arugula, Roughly Chopped

2 Medium Apple Guavas, Diced

2 Medium Ripe Avocados, Diced

1 Small Papaya, Seeded and Diced

1 8-Ounce Can Sliced Water Chestnuts, Drained and Rinsed

¼ Cup Roughly Chopped Macadamia Nuts

3 Tablespoons Lime Juice

1 Tablespoon Avocado or Olive Oil

¼ Teaspoon Salt

¼ Teaspoon Cayenne Pepper

Millionaire's Kale Salad

MAKES 3–4 SERVINGS

Greens have long been celebrated as a symbol of wealth, eaten with gusto around each New Year's Day to ensure prosperity in the days to come. Whether there's any truth in that superstition or not, you'll feel like a million bucks when you dig into this robust salad. Pomegranate arils sparkle like rubies in an emerald sea, blanketed in a creamy golden dressing. Rich in flavor and nutrition alike, this invaluable combination proves that you don't need to be a millionaire to eat like one.

First prepare the dressing by simply tossing all the ingredients into your blender or food processor and pureeing on high speed until completely smooth. You may need to pause and scrape down the sides of the container to make sure everything gets incorporated. The dressing can also be prepared in advance and stored in an airtight container in the fridge for up to two weeks.

For the salad itself, place the kale in a large bowl along with about ¼ cup of the dressing. Use your hands to "massage" the leafy greens, rubbing them firmly to break down the tough fibers. They should wilt down quite a bit to about ⅔–½ of their original volume, depending on how crisp you'd like to keep them. Add in the shredded carrots, pomegranate arils, and slivered almonds, tossing to incorporate. Pour in an additional ⅓–½ cup of the dressing, using more or less to taste, stirring thoroughly to coat all of the ingredients.

24-KARAT GOLD DRESSING:

¼ Cup Tahini

¼ Cup Carrot Juice

¼ Cup Orange Juice

¼ Cup Avocado or Olive oil

1 Clove Garlic

1 Teaspoon Dijon Mustard

½ Teaspoon Ground Ginger

½ Teaspoon Ground Turmeric

½ Teaspoon Orange Zest

½–¾ Teaspoon Salt

KALE SALAD:

1 Large Bunch (About 10–12 Ounces) Curly Kale, Stemmed and Roughly Chopped

1 Cup Shredded Carrots

½ Cup Pomegranate Arils

⅓ Cup Toasted Slivered Almonds

Go shopping through nature's jewelry box and accessorize with a new set of edible gems. Trade the pomegranate arils for blueberries, raspberries, or halved grapes to freshen up this ensemble.

Pho King Salad

When you're craving cold noodles but want the bold, distinctive flavors of Vietnamese pho, don't just settle for any limp tangle of boring rice threads; make a pho king salad. True to its name, this dish rules all other noodle salads like a boss and makes no excuses for its audacious swagger. Spike it with sriracha if you want to bring the heat without raising the temperature in the kitchen, or keep it more tame to enjoy the savory essence of hoisin and five-spice mingling amongst a forest of fresh vegetables. Perfect for those hot days when a bubbling cauldron of soup fails to appeal, there's no long-simmered stock that needs tending, so you can chill out at the dinner table instead of slaving over a hot stove.

Whisk all the ingredients for the dressing together in a small bowl, stirring until thoroughly combined. Set aside.

For the salad itself, break or cut the noodles in half because they tend to be very long. They cook almost instantly, so the key is to simply soften them rather than boil them to death. Drop them into a large pot of simmering water, use tongs to submerge and lightly stir, and cook for no more than 1 to 2 minutes. Drain and immediately rinse under cold water to stop them from becoming overcooked and mushy. They should be tender but al dente, like good angel-hair pasta. Let the noodles drain very well so as not to water down the dressing.

Transfer the drained noodles into a large bowl. Add in all of the vegetables, tofu, sprouts, herbs, and dressing, and toss everything together. It can be a bit tricky to combine since the noodles will want to stick together at first, so don't be afraid to get in there with your hands to break up the party. Once all the goodies are thoroughly distributed throughout the mixture, add sriracha to taste, and enjoy.

Veg out to add more nutrition, fresh flavors, and heartier servings. Double up on the carrots and incorporate 1 cup julienned or thinly sliced seedless cucumbers, 1½ cups shredded cabbage, and 1 cup thinly sliced red bell peppers to satisfy serious veggie lovers.

PHO-FLAVORED DRESSING:

- ¼ Cup Peanut or Avocado Oil
- 2 Tablespoons Hoisin Sauce
- 2 Tablespoons Lime Juice
- 1 Tablespoon Rice Vinegar
- 2 Teaspoons Coconut Sugar or Dark Brown Sugar, Firmly Packed
- 1 Clove Garlic, Finely Minced
- ¾ Teaspoon Salt
- ½ Teaspoon Five-Spice Powder

RICE NOODLE SALAD:

- 6.75 Ounces Thin Rice Noodles
- ⅓ Cup Sliced Fresh or Dried and Rehydrated Shiitake Mushrooms
- ½ Cup Thinly Sliced Red Onion
- ½ Cup Shredded Carrots
- 8-Ounces Fried or Baked Tofu, Thinly Sliced
- 1½ Cups Mung Bean or Soybean Sprouts
- 1½ Cups Fresh Cilantro
- ½ Cup Thai or Italian Basil
- Sriracha, to Taste (Optional)

Seared Watermelon Niçoise Salad

MAKES 4 SERVINGS

Little did I know just how controversial the ubiquitous Niçoise salad would be. Few can agree on what should be invited to join the exclusive club, aside from Niçoise olives, of course. Watermelon-based tuna is the crowning jewel of this particular interpretation, inspired by a surplus of the sweet summer fruit that prompted me to go beyond conventional preparations. It turns out that it only takes a simple sear over blistering heat to transform the juicy flesh into something of a startlingly oceanic nature. Starting with a nice firm watermelon is absolutely critical, so don't wait until the season ends and only mealy melons remain.

It might be surprising that something as wet as a watermelon can get hot enough to brown, but it has a lot of sugar that can caramelize, and when you apply moderate, even pressure with a heavy spatula (or grill weight) to compress the melon, it squeezes out enough liquid to allow the high heat to dry out the surface temporarily.

Heat a medium skillet over high heat. Add the olive oil, and when it's blisteringly hot, on the verge of smoking, carefully add the watermelon. Stand back, as it's likely to sputter angrily when the juicy melon hits the oil. Cook, pressing firmly with your spatula to gently compress the cell walls, until the watermelon has caramelized on the bottom, 2–3 minutes. Flip and repeat on the other side.

Meanwhile, prepare the dressing by simply whisking together all the ingredients, slowly streaming in the oil last to emulsify.

To make the salad itself, lay down a base of roughly torn or lightly chopped lettuce on a large serving platter and arrange the green beans, tomatoes, olives, radishes, beans, and cucumber in attractive rows. Top with the slabs of seared watermelon "tuna," drizzle the dressing generously over the whole mélange, and scatter leaves of basil on top.

> **Quick Tip:** Rather than serving up a carefully composed salad platter with ingredients arranged in perfect, neat rows, go ahead and just toss everything together. Chop the seared melon into bite-sized cubes to make sure that it gets equally distributed throughout the mix.

SEARED WATERMELON TUNA:

2 Tablespoons Olive Oil

4 (3-Inch) Squares Seedless Watermelon, Approximately 1 Inch Thick

CLASSIC VINAIGRETTE:

1 Tablespoon Finely Minced Shallot

1 Clove Garlic, Finely Minced

¼ Cup Olive Oil

2 Tablespoons Lemon Juice

1 Tablespoon Dijon Mustard

¼ Teaspoon Salt

⅛ Teaspoon Ground Black Pepper

NIÇOISE SALAD:

1 Head (10–12 Ounces) Butter or Bibb Lettuce

6 Ounces (About 1 Cup) Skinny Green Beans, Raw or Blanched (page 111)

1 Pint Grape or Cherry Tomatoes, Halved

½ Cup Pitted Niçoise Olives

6 Small Radishes, Thinly Sliced

1 Cup Cooked Cannellini Beans

1 Seedless Persian or Pickling Cucumber, Thinly Sliced

¼ Cup Fresh Basil

Sweet & Spicy Harissa Slaw

MAKES 6–8 SERVINGS

Raw carrots often get written off as nothing more than "rabbit food," but you'd never mistake this glowing ocher salad for bunny business. These crisp orange strands are hopping with an assertive harissa vinaigrette on their side, blurring the line between sweet and savory with each snappy bite. Slowly, subtly, the heat builds, leaving a satisfying afterburn in its wake. Be careful where you share this distinctive dish, because it's one of those unsuspecting starters that could very well steal the show.

In a large bowl, toss together the shredded carrots, cranberries, and walnuts to combine. Separately, whisk together the parsley, orange juice and zest, harissa, cumin, paprika, and salt. Slowly drizzle in the oil while whisking continuously, to combine and emulsify the dressing.

Pour the dressing all over the carrot mixture and toss to coat. Serve right away or let sit for the flavors to soak in until you're ready to eat. The salad can be prepared up to four days in advance and stored in an airtight container in the fridge, and is just as delicious served chilled as at room temperature.

1 Pound Shredded Carrots

½ Cup Dried Cranberries

½ Cup Chopped Toasted Walnuts

3 Tablespoons Chopped Fresh Parsley

2 Tablespoons Orange Juice

1 Tablespoon Orange Zest

1 Teaspoon Harissa

1 Teaspoon Ground Cumin

¾ Teaspoon Smoked Paprika

½ Teaspoon Salt

¼ Cup Olive Oil

Get back to your roots by seeking out other flavorful vegetable foundations for this very same slaw. Shredded sweet potatoes, beets, parsnips, radishes, or any combination of the four can lend fresh color and flavor to the mix.

Thai-Style Zucchini Ribbon Salad

Som tum, otherwise known as green papaya salad, is easily my favorite way to begin a meal. Served chilled, the crisp strands of unripe papaya are cooling, yet still pop with bursts of heat from plentiful flecks of chili peppers. Brightly acidic, tangy, and slightly salty, with just a touch of sweetness to take the edge off, every component must be in perfect balance to achieve a successful, harmonious dish.

Of course, the key ingredient, green papaya, eluded me in my limited hometown grocery stores, which is why I took a page from the ever-popular zucchini noodles that proliferate as summer brings an abundance of the green squashes. They don't stay firm as long as papaya, so just make sure you leave them undressed until the minute you're ready to serve. It may not be the genuine article, but it transports me to a delicious new world of flavor with every single bite.

For the dressing, whisk together the lime juice, coconut sugar, soy sauce, and garlic. It will seem like a lot of liquid, but don't worry, that's exactly what you want! This isn't like a traditional salad dressing; it should soak into the noodles a bit, and you will have a bit of a pool at the bottom when it's in proper proportion.

In a medium bowl, place the green beans, zucchini ribbons, and tomatoes. Pour the dressing on top and toss to coat. Add in the chili, just a little bit at a time, until it's spicy enough for your personal taste. Give it one more good toss to mix everything around and evenly distribute the ingredients before transferring everything to a serving dish. Top with a generous handful of sliced chives and chopped peanuts.

Don't let this one sit around; eat immediately!

THAI-STYLE ZUCCHINI RIBBON SALAD

- ¼ Cup Lime Juice
- 2 Tablespoons Coconut Sugar, or Dark Brown Sugar, Firmly Packed
- 2 Tablespoons Soy Sauce
- 1 Clove Garlic, Minced
- 3–4 Ounces Green Beans, Raw or Lightly Blanched*
- 2 Medium Zucchini, Spiralized or Julienned
- ½ Cup Halved Grape or Cherry Tomatoes
- ½–1 Red Thai Chili, Thinly Sliced
- Chives or Scallions, Thinly Sliced
- 2 Tablespoons Roasted and Salted Peanuts, Coarsely Chopped

Quick tip: To quickly blanch your green beans, drop them into boiling water for 30–60 seconds, until they turn bright green. Quickly plunge them into ice water to stop the cooking process. This is only necessary if your green beans are on the thicker, tougher side to begin with.

Za'atar Smashed Cucumbers

MAKES 4 SERVINGS

Ever have such a frustrating day that you feel as though you could just beat someone up? Before things get too violent, head into the kitchen to take out that aggression on your food, instead of your coworkers! Roughly bashing cucumbers rather than merely slicing them actually serves a very flavorful purpose, rather than just being a satisfying way to blow off some steam. The uneven nooks and crannies created by forcing them to split open allows them to more readily absorb dressing, whereas smooth cuts yield slick surfaces that let it roll right off. This technique is typically seen in Asian cuisine, paired with hot spices to contrast with the cooling effect of chilled cucumbers, but I love going a more Mediterranean route and hitting an herbal, savory note with fresh za'atar instead. That said, consider this a template for any sort of seasoning blend you'd prefer, from Creole seasoning to yellow curry powder. I have yet to find anything in my spice rack that clashes with the humble cucurbit!

Take a few cucumbers at a time and lay them on your cutting board. Place the blade of a wide knife (a butcher's knife is especially well suited to the task) on top and use your palm to carefully whack it, much as you would to smash garlic into paste. Continue hitting until the cucumbers split their skins. If you're worried about cutting yourself on the blade, you can use the bottom of a heavy pot or a rolling pin instead. Use your fingers to roughly tear the crushed cucumbers into bite-size pieces, working through the pile until all the vegetables have received a proper beat-down.

In a medium-sized dish, mix together all the remaining ingredients and add in the cucumbers. Toss thoroughly to coat, and serve immediately.

1 Pound Persian Cucumbers

2 Tablespoons Lemon Juice

1 Tablespoon Olive Oil

2 Tablespoons Toasted Sesame Seeds

1 Tablespoon Minced Fresh Thyme or 1 Teaspoon Dried Thyme

1 Tablespoon Minced Fresh Oregano or 1 Teaspoon Dried Oregano

2 Teaspoons Ground Sumac

¼ Teaspoon Salt

¼ Teaspoon Ground Black Pepper

Quick Tip: Reach into the pantry if you don't want to stop and chop; use half the measure of dried herbs as you would use fresh. Alternatively, put this recipe on warp speed by using about 2–3 tablespoons of a ready-made za'atar blend instead of the sesame seeds, thyme, oregano, and sumac.

Spice It Up: Substitute part or all the olive oil with chili oil for a fiery bite.

SOUPS

Chickpea Mulligatawny

MAKES 4–6 SERVINGS

Lentils are usually the star of this hot Indian stew, translated literally as "pepper water," but chickpea flour provides a handy shortcut to spicy satisfaction. Thickening in mere minutes, one bowlful could be a substantial meal all by itself, or a hearty starter for a full dinner party feast. Each batch looks massive, but you'll happily surprised if there are any leftovers to speak of once you taste this complex brew. Best of all, it keeps well and can be further stretched into additional meals with a side of cooked rice or quinoa.

Melt the coconut oil in a large stock pot over medium-high heat. Add in the onion, garlic, ginger, and salt, sautéing until softened and ever so lightly browned around the edges. Sprinkle in the curry powder and cayenne pepper to taste, depending on just how spicy you'd like it. You may want to err on the side of caution and use less to begin with, because you can always add more later on. Mix the seasonings in and cook for another 30 seconds to bring out all the rich aromas of the spices before incorporating the black pepper, shredded carrot, and apple next.

Whisk the garbanzo bean flour into the vegetable stock, stirring vigorously to make sure there are no lumps, before adding the mixture into the pot. Continue to whisk, scraping the bottom of the pan, keeping everything moving while the flour works its thickening magic. When bubbles break at a steady pace on the surface, incorporate the tomatoes, whole chickpeas, coconut milk, lime, and lemon juice. Stir thoroughly.

When the soup reaches a full boil, it should be ready to ladle out and enjoy. Top each serving with fresh cilantro and dig in!

If preparing the soup in advance, let cool before transferring to an airtight container. Store in the fridge for up to a week, and reheat gently over the stove, adding more stock as needed since it tends to continue thickening as it sits.

- 1 Tablespoon Coconut Oil
- 1 Medium Yellow Onion, Diced
- 4 Cloves Garlic, Minced
- 2 Teaspoons Grated Fresh Ginger
- 1 Teaspoon Salt
- 3–4 Tablespoons Madras Curry Powder
- ¼–½ Teaspoon Cayenne Pepper
- ½ Teaspoon Ground Black Pepper
- ½ Cup Shredded Carrot
- 1 Small Fuji Apple, Cored and Diced
- 1 Cup Garbanzo Bean Flour
- 6 Cups Vegetable Stock
- 1 (14-Ounce) Can Diced Tomatoes
- 1 (14-Ounce) Can Chickpeas, Drained and Rinsed
- 1 (14-Ounce) Can Full-Fat Coconut Milk
- 1 Tablespoon Lime Juice
- 1 Tablespoon Lemon Juice
- ½ Cup Fresh Cilantro

Quick Tip: Bring the vegetable stock and chickpea flour mixture to a boil in a separate pot while the vegetables are sautéing to finish the soup even faster.

Cucumber-Melon Gazpacho

MAKES 3–4 SERVINGS

Cucumber-melon was a hand soap, a home fragrance, or a body lotion as I knew it grow-ing up. Like many naive children failing to connect the dots to obvious relations, it took an embarrassing number of years for me to realize that it actually correlated to a potential food combination. Even then, the discovery did little to tempt my taste buds, ranking right alongside the idea of biting into a scented candle. What works for cosmetics doesn't generally merit culinary consideration, but this is one case where the two worlds collide with great success. Gazpacho is designed specifically to deliver the ultimate cooling pal-ate cleanser on a hot summer's day, which just so happens to define the essence of both cucumbers and honeydew melons as well. Mind you, this is no dessert soup, with the nota-ble twang of garlic, onions, and vinegar swimming peacefully amidst the pale green puree, but a careful balance to bridge discordant components of a menu. Making the connection between these universes was the difficult part; enjoying the results will become second nature.

Set aside about ½ cup of the diced cucumber and ¼ cup of the melon. Toss all the rest, along with the remaining ingredi-ents, into your blender or food processor and thoroughly puree, pausing to scrape down the sides of the bowl if needed, until silky smooth. Transfer to bowls and top with equal amounts of the reserved fruit and vegetable mixture, along with additional mint and sliced almonds if desired. For an extra blast of cool refreshment, pop an ice cube or two into each bowl right before serving.

The soup can be prepared up to a day in advance, stored in an airtight container in the fridge.

4 Cups (About 2 Large) Peeled and Diced English Cucumber, Divided

2 Cups (About ¼ Medium) Diced Honeydew Melon, Divided

½ Cup Toasted, Sliced Almonds

¼ Cup (About ¼ Small) Chopped Sweet Onion

1 Clove Garlic, Minced

¼ Cup Olive Oil

3 Tablespoons Sherry Vinegar

1 Tablespoon Fresh Mint Leaves (Optional)

¾ Teaspoon Salt

⅛ Teaspoon Ground White Pepper

1 Cup Water

Exploded Wonton Soup

MAKES 4–6 SERVINGS

Inspired by a true wonton wardrobe malfunction, it turns out that there's truly no need for any fussy folding. Slice the dumpling skins into strips instead, treating them like flat noodles, and you're well on your way to instant Chinese take-out gratification, with no delivery fees.

Place a large saucepan over high heat and begin sautéing the garlic and ginger in the sesame oil. The combination should become irresistibly aromatic right away. Add in the mushrooms and cabbage, cooking for 2 minutes or so until the greens wilt and mushrooms soften. Pour in a splash of broth to prevent the vegetables from burning, along with the soy sauce and vinegar. Cook for another minute longer to concentrate the savory flavors before pouring in the remainder of the broth.

Introduce the scallions and tofu, cover, and bring to a boil. Drop in the sliced wonton wrappers just a couple at a time, using your fingers to separate them before the fall into the bubbling brew. The thin dumpling skins will cook almost instantly, so take care not to overcook them into mushy gobs of dough. Allow the soup to cook for just another minute or two and serve right away. Those fragile wonton wrappers wait for no one!

1 Tablespoon Toasted Sesame Oil

3 Cloves Garlic, Minced

2 Teaspoons Grated Fresh Ginger

½ Pound Cremini or White Button Mushrooms, Thinly Sliced

1½ Cups Shredded Napa Cabbage

5 Cups Vegetable Broth

2 Tablespoons Soy Sauce

2 Teaspoons Rice Vinegar

3 Scallions, Thinly Sliced

6–8 Ounces Extra-Firm Tofu, Diced

4 Ounces Square Wonton Wrappers, Cut into ½-Inch Strips

French Onion Soup

Caramelized onions can instantly transform any dish into a memorable masterpiece, but achieving the perfect amber-brown hue can easily take upwards of 45 minutes. Coaxing out the natural sugars of the onion, slowly softening and breaking down the cell walls, you can see the Maillard reaction happen right before your eyes—but it's about as exciting as watching paint dry for all the time it takes. Traditionalists will turn up their noses at any proposed shortcuts, but even they will be won over by the stunning depth of flavor that's possible with just a bit of scientific know-how. Applying a small pinch of baking soda catapults the process forward, speeding up browning while simultaneously pummeling the onions down into a creamy puree. Though less than ideal for fabricating distinctive strands, that textural side effect turns the mixture into an instant full-bodied soup base, thick and rich without the need for added cream. Forget conventional French technique and hack your way to a stunningly complex onion soup in no time at all.

Heat the butter or oil in a large stock pot over high heat, along with the onions and garlic. Sprinkle the salt and baking soda evenly over the aromatics and start stirring. Add the bay leaf, thyme, and pepper, mixing to incorporate. Keep everything moving to prevent any one spot from getting too dark, sautéing until the mixture turns into a golden brown paste, 5–7 minutes.

Meanwhile, vigorously whisk together 2 cups of the stock, vinegar, sugar, soy sauce, and cornstarch. Make sure that there are no remaining lumps of starch before pouring the liquid mixture into a separate small saucepan over medium heat. Bring to a rolling boil, stirring periodically, until the liquid has fully thickened.

Once the onions are properly browned, pour the thickened stock mixture into the pot, scraping the bottom to pull up all the caramelized bits of onions and incorporate them into the stew. Thin with additional stock, if desired.

Enjoy with toasted slices of baguette or a sprinkle of vegan cheese for "authentic" bistro flair.

- 2 Tablespoons Vegan Butter or Olive Oil
- 3 Pounds (About 4 Large) Sweet Onions, Diced
- 3 Cloves Garlic, Minced
- ¼ Teaspoon Salt
- ⅛ Teaspoon Baking Soda
- ½ Bay Leaf, Crumbled
- 1 Teaspoon Chopped Fresh Thyme, or ½ Teaspoon Dried Thyme
- ¼ Teaspoon Ground Black Pepper
- 2–3 Cups Vegetable Stock
- 2 Tablespoons Balsamic Vinegar
- 1 Tablespoon Light Brown Sugar, Firmly Packed
- 1 Tablespoon Soy Sauce
- 1 Teaspoon Cornstarch

Garlic Bread Soup

MAKES 3–5 SERVINGS

Be it a delicate broth or thick stew, nothing completes a steaming bowlful like a hearty slice of bread. Crackling crust giving way to a spongy matrix of soft crumbs, each bite melts into submission when dipped into the soup of the day. Sometimes the soup is merely a thinly veiled excuse to reach for another helping of bread, so compellingly does that fresh loaf beckon. Let's just cut to the chase here and turn the bread into the soup itself, with a powerful blast of fresh garlic to up the ante. Save yourself the hassle of peeling the cloves by grabbing a bag of prepped garlic in advance, or going straight for a jar of minced, but don't cut back on the full measure. Garlic bread lives or dies on the pungency of that stinking rose, and once lightly caramelized in peppery olive oil, all the harsh edges will soften. Perhaps it's not fodder for a first date, but this velvety smooth base is just the beginning to a whole different sort of love affair.

Place a medium stock pot over moderate heat. Add in the oil along with the garlic, stirring frequently, until golden brown; about 3–4 minutes. Introduce the bread, paprika, and thyme next, cooking until the bread is saturated in garlicky oil. Pour in the white wine, sautéing until the liquid has evaporated. Incorporate 4½ cups of the stock, ½ teaspoon of the salt, and black pepper last, covering the pot and bringing the mixture up to a boil.

Transfer to a blender and puree until silky smooth. Add more stock and salt to taste, if needed, and ladle into bowls. Garnish with a pinch of parsley if desired.

- ¼ Cup Olive Oil
- ½ Cup (About 20 Cloves) Minced Garlic
- 6 Ounces (About 6 Slices) Sourdough or Country Bread, torn into ½-inch pieces
- 2 Teaspoons Smoked Paprika
- ½ Teaspoon Dried Thyme
- ¼ Cup Dry White Wine
- 4½–5 Cups Vegetable Stock
- ½–1 Teaspoon Salt
- ½ Teaspoon Ground Black Pepper
- 1 Tablespoon Chopped Fresh Parsley (Optional)

Instant Kimchi Noodle Soup

MAKES 4–6 SERVINGS

Like many penniless, voracious college students, instant ramen saw me through many late night study sessions back in the day. When the fridge was empty and the pantry otherwise bare, I could always count on a packet or two of freeze-dried noodles to see me through the lean times. They still hold a special place in my heart—the mere thought of those chewy wheat strands swimming in a salty sea of vegetable broth sends my head spinning with hunger—but I'd like to think that my palate has evolved quite a bit since then. Now my approach is a good deal spicier, fresher, and undoubtedly healthier. No longer shackled to those quick-cooking fried noodle bricks, I've found that buckwheat soba takes only a minute or two longer to reach al dente perfection while adding depth and a pleasant earthiness to the entire bowl. Kimchi is the star of the show here, so even if you don't have all the vegetables suggested below, you can easily make up the difference by just piling on the peppery pickled cabbage instead.

Bring a large saucepan of water to a boil over high heat. Add the soba noodles and cook until just tender, about 3–4 minutes. Drain and immediately rinse with cold water to prevent them from getting mushy. Set aside.

Meanwhile, pile the kimchi, all the vegetables, soy sauce, instant wakame flakes, and tofu into a large pot along with the broth. Cover and set over high heat on the stove. Bring to a boil, reduce heat to keep the liquid at a lively simmer, and cook just until the vegetables are tender and the tofu has absorbed the flavorful stock.

Divide the noodles evenly between 4 or 6 bowls, depending on how many mouths you have to feed (or how hungry you are.) Ladle the soup on top and serve right away. The soup itself can be made in advance and kept in the fridge for up to three days as long as the noodles are kept separate. Buckwheat isn't as resilient as plain wheat and will quickly become gummy as it sits in the broth.

4 Ounces Dry Soba Noodles

2 Cups Drained Vegan Kimchi,* Plus ½ Cup Brine

4 Scallions, Sliced

2 Tablespoons Soy Sauce

1 Tablespoon Instant Wakame Flakes

½ Cup Sliced Cremini or Button Mushrooms

1 Small Zucchini, Halved and Thinly Sliced

¾ Pound Firm Tofu, Diced

6 Cups Mushroom or Vegetable Broth

Kimchi is traditionally fermented over the course of several days, if not weeks, but you can whip up a satisfying quick-fix imitation with a bit of ingenuity and a few basic kitchen staples. Roughly chop a head of Napa cabbage and plunge it into boiling water for 5–6 minutes, until tender, then quickly rinse under cold water. Toss it into a large bowl with 2 tablespoons chile paste or sriracha, 2 tablespoons rice vinegar, 1 tablespoon soy sauce, 3 or 4 chopped scallions, and 1 teaspoon each garlic powder and ginger powder. Mix it all aggressively with your hands to further break down and soften the cabbage. Feel free to add in extra vegetables like sliced radishes, carrots, or cucumbers to liven up the mix, too. Since this is not an actual pickle, it will only keep in the fridge for 1–2 weeks in an airtight container.

Manhattan Mushroom Chowder

MAKES 4–6 SERVINGS

Creamy New England-style chowder is the type that most people think of when the seafood stew comes to mind. Lesser known but every bit as comforting is the Manhattan-style chowder, which ditches the creamy base in favor of tomatoes with a spicy kick. Mushrooms take the place of seafood in my untraditional approach, lending full-bodied umami flavor and toothsome, meaty texture throughout the entire comforting brew. Long-simmered flavor is instantly replicated with the robust, smoky char of fire-roasted tomatoes, unleashed with the mere twist of a can opener. It's just the thing to chase away the chill of winter, or simply provide a spoonful of comfort on a gloomy day.

Combine the oil, onion, celery, garlic, and carrots in a large stock pot over medium-high heat. Sauté until the vegetables have softened and begin taking on a bit of brownness around the edges. Add in the mushrooms along with ½ teaspoon of salt to help draw out more of their moisture, helping the cooking process along while preventing them from burning. Stir in all the herbs, spices, and the tomato paste, continuing to stir and sauté for another minute or two. You want to slightly caramelize the tomato paste to enhance its natural umami notes, but be careful not to take it too far. Add splashes of the stock if it threatens to stick or burn on the bottom.

Add in the diced tomatoes, liquid and all, followed by the shredded potatoes. Stir well, cover, and reduce the heat to medium. By the time the mixture comes up to a rapid boil, the potatoes should be tender and the whole brew irresistibly aromatic. Slowly pour in the remaining stock until it reaches your ideal thickness.

Ladle into bowls and serve with oyster crackers or crusty bread on the side, if desired.

3 Tablespoons Olive Oil

1 Cup (About 1 Medium) Diced Yellow Onion

½ Cup (1–2 Stalks) Diced Celery

4 Cloves Garlic, Minced

1 Cup Shredded Carrots

¾ Pound (About 4 Cups) Roughly Chopped Cremini or Button Mushrooms

½–1 Teaspoon Salt

1½ Teaspoons Dried Thyme

½ Teaspoon Celery Seeds

½ Teaspoon Dried Marjoram

½ Teaspoon Crushed Red Pepper Flakes

1 Bay Leaf, Crumbled

¼ Cup Tomato Paste

2–3 Cups Mushroom or Vegetable Stock

2 (14-Ounce) Cans Fire-Roasted Diced Tomatoes

1 Cup Frozen Shredded Potatoes (Unseasoned Hash Browns), Thawed

Pozole Verde

Tomatoes are a lovable but bossy bunch. Everyone cheers when summer breaks and they proliferate across produce bins near and far, inspiring reverence that extends far beyond the table. Poetry has been written, wars have been fought over—and with—them, and even now that they're hardly a rarefied luxury, their popularity shows no signs of flagging. I adore tomatoes just as much as the next cook, but sometimes it's nice to give them the day off. While typically the dominant flavor in Mexican pozole, draining the red of the tomatoes away leaves a verdant green stew in its wake. Leaning more heavily on a smattering of herbaceous cilantro and the tart tomatillos found in spicy salsa verde, it's easier to taste the corn of the jumbo hominy kernels, the essential ingredient that truly defines this stew.

Place a large stock pot over medium heat on the stove and add in the oil. Begin to sauté ¼ cup of the onion along with the jalapeno, adding more or less based on your spice preference, and 3½ cups of the cabbage. Cook until the onions are translucent and the vegetables softened; about 3 minutes. Sprinkle in the cumin, oregano, and black pepper, stirring to combine, and sauté for another minute for them to release their full flavors. Quickly add the salsa to prevent anything from burning, followed by the vegetable stock. Incorporate the beans and hominy next, stirring well. Cover and raise the heat to high, bringing the mixture up to a boil.

Remove the lid and continue to simmer until the cabbage is tender, 3–4 minutes. Turn off the heat before stirring in the cilantro.

To serve, ladle into bowls and top with the remaining chopped onion, cabbage, sliced radishes, and avocado.

- 1 Tablespoon Olive Oil
- ½ Cup Diced Yellow Onion, Divided
- ½–1 Jalapeño, Minced
- 4 Cups (About 1 Pound) Shredded Green Cabbage, Divided
- ½ Teaspoon Ground Cumin
- ½ Teaspoon Dried Oregano
- ½ Teaspoon Ground Black Pepper
- 16 Ounces (2 Cups) Salsa Verde
- 2 Cups Vegetable Stock
- 1 (15-Ounce Can) or 1½ Cups Cooked Pinto Beans, Rinsed and Drained
- 1 (15-ounce) Can White Hominy, Rinsed and Drained
- 1 Cup Fresh Cilantro, Roughly Chopped
- 3–4 Thinly Sliced Radishes
- 1–2 Medium Ripe Avocados, Sliced

Silky Matcha Miso Soup

MAKES 2–3 SERVINGS

Miso soup should be a staple for any busy cook for its endlessly accommodating, infallible base. Got a handful of tired, limp carrots? Wilting greens? Wrinkled squash that have seen better days? Chop them up and toss them in; everyone's welcome to this party. A spoonful of miso paste, light, dark, soybean, or chickpea, brings everything together in a revitalizing hot brew. While you can't go wrong with this approach, I'd wager that with a bit more intention, you can do a whole lot better. Jazz things up with the depths of different mushrooms and add more body with soymilk instead of plain water. Matcha lends a subtle edge of bitterness, complemented by the natural sweetness of creamy pureed pear. It's not what most people would imagine when conjuring up visions of miso soup, which makes this unexpected variation a particularly gratifying way to break through the same old miso monotony.

Place the water, shiitake mushrooms, and chopped pear in a medium saucepan over high heat. Cover and bring to a boil. Simmer for just a minute or two, until the pear is fork-tender. Remove the mushroom caps and slice into ¼-inch strips when they're cool enough to handle.

Meanwhile, transfer the pear and liquid to your blender along with the soymilk, miso paste, and matcha. Puree until completely smooth, and return the mixture to the saucepan. Place over medium heat and introduce the instant wakame, fresh mushroom, and yuba or tofu. Cook just until the mushrooms have softened slightly and the soup is piping hot. Re-introduce the sliced shiitake, top with scallion, and serve at once.

2 Cups Water

3 Dried Shiitake Mushroom Caps

1 Ripe Pear, Peeled, Cored, and Chopped

1 Cup Unsweetened Soymilk

3 Tablespoons Sweet White Miso Paste

1 Teaspoon Matcha Powder

1 Tablespoon Instant Wakame Flakes

4 Ounces Buna-Shimeji (Brown Beech Mushrooms) or Enoki Mushrooms

2–3 Ounces Yuba, Thinly Sliced, or Soft Tofu, Cubed

1 Scallion, Thinly Sliced

Spinach and Artichoke Bisque

MAKES 4–6 SERVINGS

It's just not a party until someone brings the artichoke dip. Commanding far more attention than any of the crudités or crackers, it's always the first thing to go. The accoutrements are really just vehicles for delivering as much dip as possible in each bite anyway; if you simply put out spoons, I have no doubt that guests would happily go to town without any formalities. This creamy soup is proof of exactly that, converting the time-honored starter into a main event. You could always serve fresh cut vegetables or crisp toast on the side for the sake of nostalgia, but no one will complain as long as there's plenty of this devilishly rich vegetable soup to go around.

To begin, make a thick cashew cream by placing the cashews and 1 cup of the vegetable stock in your blender. Crank it up to high speed and thoroughly puree, until completely silky smooth. It may take up to 3 minutes at full blast, so you can get started on the soup itself in the meantime.

Heat the oil in a large stock pot over medium-high heat. Sauté the onion, garlic, and artichoke hearts until softened and lightly browned around the edges, 4–5 minutes. Add 2 cups of the remaining vegetable broth, the spinach, ¾ of the cashew cream, tarragon, marjoram, and pepper. Bring the mixture just to the brink of a boil.

Use an immersion blender to puree about half of the soup, or transfer ½ of the soup to your blender and thoroughly puree before stirring back into the stock pot. Thin with the remaining stock until it reaches your desired consistency. Ladle into bowls and swirl the reserved cashew cream on top. Serve piping hot.

¾ Cup Raw Cashews

3–4 Cups Vegetable Stock, Divided

1 Tablespoon Olive Oil

1 Small Yellow Onion, Diced

2 Cloves Garlic, Minced

2 14.5-Ounce Jars Marinated Artichoke Hearts, Rinsed and Drained

10 Ounces Frozen Spinach, Thawed

½ Teaspoon Dried Tarragon

½ Teaspoon Dried Marjoram

⅛ Teaspoon Ground Black Pepper

Quick Tip: Cashews do all the heavy lifting for the savory base, but in case your blender isn't powerful enough to fully puree the nuts, you can mix in about ¾ cup of raw cashew butter instead.

Go ahead, get cheesy! Melt in ½–1 cup shredded vegan cheese for some extra gooey goodness.

Tamarind Rasam

MAKES 2–3 SERVINGS

Found in giant roiling vats across the nation, the classic Chinese approach is most famous and beloved for good reason, but nearly every culture has its own delicious take on hot and sour soup. Rasam comes to us by way of India, and has as many variations as there are days in the year. Every cook worth their salt will argue that theirs (or their mother's) is the best, the most authentic, the only true form of the concept, but it's nothing more than bravado talking. The only unassailable rule to rasam is that it must contain hot spices and liquid. Seriously, it's that simple! My favorite variation emphasizes tamarind rather than vinegar for a unique, irreplaceable tangy bite that sets it apart from Asian interpretations. This brothy, spicy brew is a great way to kick off a meal, waking up your taste buds with each punchy, piquant spoonful.

Heat the oil in a medium saucepan over medium heat. Add the minced garlic and coriander seeds. As they start to sputter and sizzle, add the tomato, stir vigorously to prevent anything from sticking to the bottom of the pan, and then follow with the cumin, black pepper, red pepper, and turmeric. Cook for about a minute, until highly aromatic.

Separately, whisk together the stock and tamarind paste, making sure that the paste has fully dissolved into the liquid. Pour the mixture into the pan, stirring and scraping the bottom to incorporate all the spices, and season with salt. Cover and bring to a boil.

The soup is ready to serve as soon as it's bubbling hot. Ladle into bowls and garnish with cilantro to serve.

2 Teaspoons Coconut or Peanut Oil

2 Cloves Garlic, Finely Minced

¼ Teaspoon Whole Coriander Seed

1 Large Tomato, Diced (About 1 Cup)

1 Teaspoon Ground Cumin

½ Teaspoon Ground Black Pepper

¼ Teaspoon Crushed Red Pepper Flakes

⅛ Teaspoon Ground Turmeric

2 Cups Vegetable Stock

1 Tablespoon Tamarind Paste

¼ Teaspoon Salt

2 Tablespoons Fresh Cilantro, Finely Chopped

Three Pea Soup

MAKES 2–4 SERVINGS

When the apocalypse finally comes, there will be two things left: Cockroaches and canned pea soup. The murky, swampy stew that emerges from those metal coffins is somewhere between the realm of liquid and solid, as undefinable as it is unrecognizable as actual edible material. Everyone has it, lurking in the back of their pantries in case of some unspecified "emergency," but the real crisis would be if someone dared to consume that sludge. Stop the madness and give peas a chance! Start with verdant whole peas, rather than overboiled split peas, and you're already ahead of the game. Light, bright vegetables and fresh herbs revive the standard, stagnant blend, and a triple dose of pea power really drives the concept home. It won't stick around nearly as long as those ancient tins . . . and that's a very good thing, indeed.

Heat the oil in a medium stock pot over moderate heat and add in the diced shallots. Sauté for a minute or so until translucent and add in the vegetable stock, peas, and fennel. Cover and bring to a boil. Simmer for just another minute or two, double check that the fennel is fork-tender, and immediately turn off the heat.

Transfer about ¾ of the mixture to your blender. Introduce the spinach, dill, cashew butter, and salt. Puree on high speed, until completely smooth. Return the blend to the pot and mix in the remainder. Alternatively, blend the whole batch for a completely silky soup.

To make the salad, simply toss together all the ingredients and top bowls of soup with equally sized servings. Enjoy right away, while still piping hot.

SPRING PEA SOUP:

- **1 Tablespoon Olive Oil**
- **2 Medium Shallots, Diced**
- **3 Cups Vegetable Stock**
- **3 Cups Frozen Peas, Thawed**
- **1 Medium Bulb Fennel, Fronds Removed, Finely Diced (About 2 Cups)**
- **1 Cup Fresh Baby Spinach, Lightly Packed**
- **2 Tablespoons Fresh Dill, Roughly Chopped**
- **2 Tablespoons Raw Cashew Butter**
- **½ Teaspoon Salt**

SNOW PEA SALAD:

- **1 Tablespoon Lemon Juice**
- **1 Teaspoon Olive Oil**
- **1 Cup Snow Peas, Sliced**
- **½ Cup Pea Shoots or Sprouts**

Quick Tip: Prepare this soup in advance and serve it chilled on particularly sweltering days.

SIDES

Blistered Citrus Snap Peas

MAKES 2–3 SERVINGS

Snow peas used to be the only podded legume for me. Thin, delicate green planks that erupted across the miles of twisting vines that proliferated in our otherwise sparse garden, its sheer abundance meant there was never any reason to venture beyond this glorious green vegetable. The snow peas were always the first vegetables to emerge and welcome each new spring season, heralding brighter days and more bountiful harvests to come.

Now that garden of my childhood is thousands of miles away, sounding like little more than a dream. Farmers' markets have come to replace those homegrown goodies, shaking up the standard bill of fare with their comparatively endless, irresistible range of fresh temptations. Graduating to the thicker, juicier, dare I say, meatier podded delights known as snap peas, I relish snacking on them raw or simply seared. Tossed in a blistering hot pan with a splash of oil and a kiss of zesty citrus and spice, their inherent sweetness truly shines through after a scant minute on the fire.

Heat the oil in a medium skillet over high heat and wait until it becomes so hot that it makes you nervous, just before it starts smoking. Toss in the snap peas, cooking quickly on all sides until the pods are bright green and lightly charred. Turn off the heat, toss in the remaining seasonings, and serve immediately.

1 Tablespoon Olive Oil

¾ Pound Fresh Snap Peas, Trimmed if Necessary

1 Teaspoon Lemon Zest

1 Teaspoon Orange Zest

½ Teaspoon Grapefruit Zest

½ Teaspoon Black Pepper

½ Teaspoon Salt

Cauliflower Risotto alla Milanese

MAKES 3–4 SERVINGS

Folklore warns that proper risotto must be stirred continuously for a full 30 minutes or more, using only the most finicky varieties of short grain rice. It's time to debunk that antiquated myth and rethink that painstaking approach. Cauliflower transforms into an impressive dupe for rice, cutting down on the cooking time and blending into a creamy puree that negates need for the typical additions of cream and cheese. Luxurious strands of saffron impart a golden glow to this study in elegant simplicity, creamy and comforting yet impossibly light. It's come a long way from its Italian roots, but still has the same heart and soul.

Heat the oil in a large saucepan with the shallot, and sauté over high heat until golden brown. Quickly deglaze with the wine, let simmer for about 1 minute to burn off the harsh bite of the alcohol, and then add in all the remaining ingredients. Let cook until the cauliflower pieces are cooked but still toothsome, stirring periodically to prevent it from burning, 5–7 minutes. Most if not all the liquid should have absorbed.

Transfer about ⅓ of the mixture to your blender or food processor and thoroughly puree, until completely smooth. Pour the puree back into the saucepan and stir well. Adjust seasonings to taste if needed and serve while piping hot.

3 Tablespoons Olive Oil

1 Medium Shallot, Minced

¼ Cup Dry White Wine

1 Pound "Riced" Cauliflower*

1 Cup Vegetable Stock

2 Tablespoons Nutritional Yeast

1 Tablespoon White Miso Paste

¼ Teaspoon Saffron

½ Teaspoon Ground Black Pepper

*Cauliflower can be transformed into vegetable-based "rice" in 60 seconds flat by chopping the raw florets and tossing them into your food processor. Pulse, pausing to scrape down the sides of the bowl as needed, until the cauliflower is broken down to a coarse, slightly chunky dice, about the size of small grains. If your cauliflower is particularly large or your food processor somewhat small, you may need to do this in batches.

Quick Tip: Save time by preparing the riced cauliflower in advance and storing it in the freezer until needed. No need to thaw; just toss it into the hot pan and get cooking! You can also find ready-riced cauliflower in many grocery stores now in the same general area as the salad kits.

Need a non-alcoholic alternative? Just use more vegetable stock instead of white wine.

Couscous-a-Roni

MAKES 4–6 SERVINGS

It's not the original San Francisco treat, but I daresay this homemade rendition is far better than anything you'd find in a box. Replacing the rice with couscous allows it to cook in half the time as the original, and quality ingredients ensure a far richer flavor. Though it may not look like anything special at first glance, that's exactly the beauty of this dish; that neutrality allows it to play nicely with any entree, and even the pickiest eaters will gobble it right up.

Heat the oil in a large saucepan over medium-high heat. Add in the onion and garlic, sautéing for a minute until softened and aromatic. Introduce the orzo next, stirring periodically until the pasta is toasted and golden brown. Pour in the broth along with the soy sauce, parsley, and couscous. Cover and bring up to a rapid boil. Reduce the heat to maintain a gentle simmer until the liquid is mostly absorbed, about 7 minutes.

Remove the pan from the heat but keep the lid on, letting the pasta steam for another minute or two. Fluff with a fork before serving.

3 Tablespoons Olive Oil
1 Yellow Onion, Minced
1 Clove Garlic, Minced
¾ Cup Orzo Pasta
3 Cups Vegetable Broth
1 Teaspoon Soy Sauce
1 Teaspoon Dried Parsley
1 Cup Couscous

The pasta-bilities are endless! Any other small, quick-cooking shape such as ditalini, pastina, stelline, or broken spaghetti could be swapped in for the orzo for visual and textural variety.

Cruciferous Colcannon

MAKES 3–4 SERVINGS

For a delicious twist on the Irish staple, mashed broccoli and cauliflower join forces with kale, cabbage, and horseradish in this harmonious family reunion. They're all cruciferous vegetables, and all pitch-perfect when singing together as a modern ode to the beloved Emerald Isle staple. It will be hard to go back to plain old mashed potatoes once this fresh blend has graced your table.

Heat the oil in a large saucepan over medium heat. Add the kale and cabbage in handfuls, stirring until wilted down enough to comfortably accommodate all the green. Toss in the scallions and sauté for two more minutes to soften. Introduce the cauliflower and broccoli next, along with the vegetable stock. Cook for 4–5 minutes, until the vegetables are fork-tender.

Remove the vegetables from the heat and roughly mash with a potato masher. Add in the nutritional yeast, horseradish, salt, and nutmeg, stirring, folding, and mashing until the whole mixture is completely combined, creamy, and well seasoned. Transfer to a serving dish and for an extra indulgent finishing touch, top with thick pat of vegan butter melting luxuriously over the whole mound.

2 Tablespoons Olive Oil

2 Cups Stemmed and Chopped Kale

2 Cups Shredded Savoy or Green Cabbage

3 Scallions, Thinly Sliced

½ Pound Frozen Cauliflower, Thawed

½ Pound Frozen Broccoli, Thawed

¼ Cup Vegetable Stock

1 Tablespoon Nutritional Yeast

2 Teaspoons Freshly Grated Horseradish

¾ Teaspoon Salt

⅛ Teaspoon Ground Nutmeg

Vegan Butter, to Serve (Optional)

Quick Tip: You can even use frozen kale! Check your local grocery store's freezer section, and you might be happily surprised about the abundance of prepared greens stashed away amongst the typical vegetable options. To keep things fresh and exciting, consider mixing up the greens; spinach is always a solid option.

Fresh Corn Grits

Rather than making grits from dried cornmeal, my version is more like a cross between polenta and creamed corn, utilizing fresh, coarsely pureed corn for a brighter, lighter flavor. Riffing on the classic southern staple of shrimp and grits, my favorite way to serve up this summery side dish is with any sort of imitation crustaceans, be it konjac or soy-based, lightly pan-fried with a generous dose of garlic. You certainly don't need fake shrimp to enjoy it, though; a bit of baked tofu would also make for a stellar accompaniment, but all you really need is a spoon.

Melt your butter or coconut oil in a sauté pan over medium-high heat, and swirl in the olive oil. Add the shallot and cook for 2 minutes, stirring frequently, until softened. Incorporate the agave and corn next, sautéing for about 5–7 more minutes to soften the corn and enhance its natural sweetness. It shouldn't change the color much so don't worry if you don't see any browning.

Transfer everything into your blender or food processor, along with ¾ cup of the nondairy milk and nutritional yeast, and pulse in short bursts until the mixture is creamy, but still has a good bit of texture to it. Drizzle in more nondairy milk if needed, to reach your desired consistency. Add salt and pepper, stir to incorporate, and adjust seasonings to taste if needed.

The grits can be prepared in advance if stored in an airtight container in the fridge. You may need to add more nondairy milk when reheating, because it thickens significantly as it sits.

- 1 Tablespoon Vegan Butter or Coconut Oil
- 1 Tablespoon Olive Oil
- 1 Large Shallot or ½ Small Yellow Onion, Diced
- 1 Teaspoon Light Agave Nectar
- 3 Cups Fresh or Frozen Corn Kernels, Thawed
- ¾–1 Cup Unsweetened, Plain Nondairy Milk
- 2 Tablespoons Nutritional Yeast
- ½ Teaspoon Salt
- ⅛ Teaspoon Ground Black Pepper

Hasselback Zucchini

MAKES 6 SERVINGS

There was a brief moment in recent history when hasselback potatoes went from an obscure culinary concept to the hottest food trend exploding on the social media scene. Particularly when Thanksgiving rolled around, these thinly semi-sliced potatoes were inescapable, ranking right up there with bacon and sriracha. Combining crispy ridges with tender, fluffy interiors, they deserved the acclaim as better baked potatoes, but their brilliance can't be rushed. From oven to table, we're talking 1–2 hours of cook time. Luckily, potatoes aren't the only vegetable that can enjoy this technique; zucchini is a breath of fresh air in this overwhelming sea of starch. Choose smaller squash to ensure quick cooking times and cut consistent, wafer-thin slices for the best results.

Preheat your oven to 500°F.

Properly prepping the zucchini is essential for success here, so be careful when cutting. You don't want to go all the way through the vegetables, but just about ¾ of the way, at regularly spaced intervals of just a few millimeters. Exact measurements aren't critical as long as you're consistent. For those less confident with their knife skills, try placing thin skewers or dowels on either side of the zucchini to prevent the blade from going all the way down to the cutting board.

Place the zucchini on a lightly greased baking sheet and drizzle liberally with oil. Combine the garlic, thyme, rosemary, red pepper flakes, and salt together and smear this mixture all over, pushing it in between the cut layers and all over the sides. Cover loosely with foil and slide the pan into the hot oven.

Lift the foil after about 6 minutes to check on their progress. The zucchini should be just about fork-tender. Bake for an additional 2 minutes or so, uncovered, until lightly browned. Serve warm.

1½ Pounds (About 6 Small) Zucchini

2 Tablespoons Olive Oil

3 Cloves Garlic, Finely Minced

½ Teaspoon Dried Thyme

½ Teaspoon Dried Rosemary

½ Teaspoon Crushed Red Pepper Flakes

½ Teaspoon Salt

Spice things up by swapping in equal measures of any dried herbs, or up to 2 teaspoons of your favorite seasoning mixture for new flavor adventures. Try a bright, zingy lemon-pepper variation by using 1 teaspoon dried parsley, 1 teaspoon fresh lemon zest, and ½ teaspoon ground black pepper, just for starters.

My Big Fat Greek Asparagus

MAKES 3–4 SERVINGS

For years, pencil-thin, spindly stalks of asparagus were the only respectable option for any serious chef, buying into the notion that anything more voluptuous would be tough or "woody." Not only is that a fallacy, but a woeful waste of the best produce that spring has to offer. Thick, juicy spears bear a much fuller flavor in each bite, providing ample surface area to cover in more robust seasonings that would otherwise smoother those twiggy specimens. Briny Kalamata olives, sun-dried tomatoes, and fresh dill celebrate this seasonal treat with a touch of Greek flair, dressing the once maligned stalks in a shapely and bold new style. That all said, age determines texture more than width, so freshness will always trump shape or size, and at the end of the day, all asparagus are still beautiful. Cook thinner asparagus for only 3–5 minutes, if that's all you can find.

Set a large skillet over medium-high heat and add in the oil. Once the surface begins to shimmer, introduce the asparagus. Sauté for 6–7 minutes, until bright green and fork-tender yet still crisp.

Meanwhile toss all the remaining ingredients into your food processor and pulse to combine. Pause to scrape down the sides of the bowl if necessary, chopping the mixture into a coarse tapenade, with plenty of chunky bites remaining.

Transfer the cooked asparagus to a serving platter and top with the olive mixture. Enjoy hot, or prepare in advance and chill for a more refreshing spring side. Once cooled, it also travels well, making it an excellent picnic guest!

1 Tablespoons Olive Oil

1 Pound Trimmed Asparagus

⅓ Cup Pitted Kalamata Olives

¼ Cup Sun-dried Tomatoes

3 Tablespoons Fresh Dill

1 Tablespoon Red Wine Vinegar

1 Clove Garlic

¼ Teaspoon Dried Oregano

¼ Teaspoon Dried Thyme

¼ Teaspoon Ground Black Pepper

Pan-Fried Balsamic Brussels Sprouts

MAKES 2–4 SERVINGS

Some recipes are dangerous, and not for the bodily harm they might inflict. Though that could be true for typical fried brussels sprouts, moving them out of the deep fryer and into a heavy skillet turns them into an entirely different hazard. Even for supposed sprout-haters, these particularly tiny cabbages are so utterly irresistible, it's impossible not to polish off a full batch in one sitting, no matter how few diners are present. Searing them in blazing hot oil quickly darkens their exteriors to a devilishly dark and nutty char while dialing down their otherwise pungent bite. The key here is to use only the very smallest of sprouts to ensure that they cook all the way through. You might as well stock up next time you shop; it will be hard to go back to any other slower, less satisfying cooking methods after you give this a go.

Place a heavy-bottomed skillet over high heat. While it heats, toss the brussels sprouts, oil, balsamic vinegar, maple syrup, salt, and pepper together in a large bowl, coating the vegetable thoroughly. Once the pan is screaming hot, dump in sprouts all at once, standing back slightly in case it might spit and sputter. No matter how badly you might want to stir, resist the impulse and don't even think about touching that pan for 5 minutes! This will ensure a nice, dark crust forms on the outsides.

Use a wide spatula to flip the brussels sprouts over and cook the opposite sides until similarly browned, 3–4 minutes. Some of the leaves will be charred dark brown or even black, but that's exactly what you want to see. The sprouts should all be fork-tender and ready to serve right away. Top with a sprinkle of toasted almonds, if desired.

1 Pound Small Brussels Sprouts, Halved

¼ Cup Olive Oil

2 Tablespoons Balsamic Vinegar

1 Tablespoon 100% Grade B Maple Syrup

½ Teaspoon Salt

¼ Teaspoon Ground Black Pepper

¼ Cup Toasted, Slivered Almonds (Optional)

Smoky Chipotle Creamed Kale

MAKES 3–4 SERVINGS

The 1950s called; they want their creamed spinach back. In the early, dark ages of American cuisine, it was unleashed upon the masses in steakhouses as a feeble attempt to entice vegetable-phobic diners to eat their greens. One order would contain far more heavy cream than anything resembling spinach, fresh or otherwise. Rather than covering such tender greens up, disguising them in a cloak of dairy, I'd like to think of the little leaves as a "splurge" in and of themselves. Opting for more hearty but still tender baby kale, this plant-powered side dish doesn't shy away from the spice, adopting a smoky accent of adobo sauce, harmonizing with the savory, tropical notes of coconut milk, rather than straight cream. These are greens you'll actually want to eat, no matter how you typically feel about kale OR spinach.

Melt the coconut oil in a medium skillet over moderate heat. Add the shallot, ¼ teaspoon salt, and the chipotle. Cook, stirring frequently, until the shallots have softened and the mixture is aromatic, 2–3 minutes.

Meanwhile, whisk the coconut milk together with the adobo sauce, cornstarch, paprika, and maple syrup. Beat vigorously to ensure that there are no clumps of cornstarch remaining before pouring the mixture into the hot skillet. Turn up the heat slightly to medium-high and cook, stirring occasionally, until the sauce has thickened.

Introduce the baby kale in batches, fold it in until the full measure fits into the skillet, cooking just until it wilts down but is still bright green and tender. Incorporate the vinegar and season with additional salt to taste, if desired. Serve hot.

- 1 Teaspoon Coconut Oil
- 1 Large Shallot, Finely Diced
- ¼–½ Teaspoon Salt
- 1 Canned Chipotle in Adobo, Finely Chopped
- 1 (14-Ounce) Can Full-Fat Coconut Milk
- 1 Tablespoon Canned Adobo Sauce
- 2 Tablespoons Cornstarch
- 1 Teaspoon Smoked Paprika
- 1 Tablespoon 100% Grade B Maple Syrup
- 1 Pound Baby Kale
- 2 Tablespoons Malt or Sherry Vinegar

There's no reason why kale should get all the glory. Go ahead and experiment with other dark, leafy greens, like chopped collards or Swiss chard. Just add them in at the same time as the coconut mixture, since they're somewhat heartier than baby kale. If using standard curly or dinosaur kale, the same advice for timing applies as well.

Sweet Potato Cacio e Pepe

MAKES 3–4 SERVINGS

Silky spirals of tender sweet potato unfurl themselves in cashew-based cream sauce, splattered with flecks of black pepper so fierce that you'd swear it could bite back. This is the new face of cacio e pepe, unencumbered by the heaviness of butter or intolerably unctuous cheese. Rather than weighing you down, each punchy, luscious forkful should wake you up!

Select thicker sweet potatoes for greater spiralizing success; skinny tubers are tough to turn into noodles. Alternatively, use an everyday vegetable peeler to make wide ribbons instead.

Spiralize the sweet potatoes, discarding or reserving the long "cores" for another use. Heat the oil in a large skillet over medium heat and add in the sweet potato strands. Cook, stirring gently so as not to break up the spirals, for just a minute or two.

Meanwhile, whisk together ⅓ cup of the vegetable stock, nutritional yeast, cashew butter, pepper, and salt. If you have trouble getting the mixture to emulsify, toss it into your blender and pulse for a few seconds until smooth. Pour the sauce into the pan, stirring to coat the noodles, and bring to a simmer. Continue to cook, stirring periodically, until the sweet potato is fork-tender; about 5–6 minutes. Drizzle in additional vegetable stock if needed, to keep the sauce smooth. Serve hot.

1 Pound Sweet Potatoes, Peeled

2 Tablespoons Olive Oil

⅓–½ Cup Vegetable Stock

¼ Cup Nutritional Yeast

1 Tablespoon Raw Cashew Butter

1 Teaspoon Ground Black Pepper

½ Teaspoon Salt

Quick Tip: If you can't take the heat, don't turn on the stove; use zucchini instead of sweet potatoes to skip the cooking altogether! Simply blend the ingredients for the sauce but withhold the vegetable broth at first. Toss it with the "noodles," slowly drizzling it in until you're satisfied with the consistency. Serve immediately, before the zucchini begins to soften.

ENTRÉES

Artichoke Barbacoa

MAKES 3–5 SERVINGS

Celebrating Taco Tuesdays has forced me to consider more creative ways to dress up stacks of tortillas than the standard black bean default. There's nothing wrong with playing the classic hits every now and then, but with 52 opportunities to throw down every year, those same old songs become tiresome in no time at all. Artichoke is one unconventional ingredient that doesn't get much respect as a main dish, let alone a robust Mexican mock meat, but it's the secret ingredient sure to revolutionize the weekly routine.

Barbacoa is best served simply, over warm corn tortillas with sharp diced onions, fresh cilantro, and a squeeze of lime juice for contrast. That said, a spoonful of guacamole or salsa certainly wouldn't hurt.

Heat the oil in a medium saucepan over moderate heat, adding the garlic and chipotle when hot. Sauté for a minute or two until the spicy aroma fills the kitchen. Stir in the bay leaf, cumin, oregano, pepper, salt, and cloves, extracting their full flavor with another minute on the heat. Quickly deglaze the pan with the vegetable stock, scraping up all the caramelized spices on the bottom of the pan. Follow that addition with the vinegar, lime juice, and artichoke hearts.

Get in there and stir aggressively, using your spatula to smash and break apart the artichokes so that the texture resembles something like shredded meat. It may be a bit tough at first but will continue to soften as it cooks. Continue mixing and mashing for 6–8 minutes, until the artichoke is tender, beaten into submission, and has absorbed all the excess liquid.

Serve on corn tortillas and top with diced onion, fresh cilantro, and a squeeze of lime juice, to taste.

ARTICHOKE BARBACOA:

1 Tablespoon Olive Oil

1 Clove Garlic, Minced

1 Canned Chipotle in Adobo, Minced

1 Small Bay Leaf, Crumbled

1 Teaspoon Ground Cumin

½ Teaspoon Oregano

¼ Teaspoon Ground Black Pepper

¼ Teaspoon Salt

⅛ Teaspoon Ground Cloves

¼ Cup Vegetable Stock

2 Tablespoons Apple Cider Vinegar

1 Tablespoon Lime Juice

12 Ounces Frozen Artichoke Hearts, Thawed

TO SERVE:

8–10 (5- or 6-Inch) Corn Tortillas

½ Cup Diced Sweet Onion

½ Cup Fresh Cilantro

1 Lime

Cashew Scampi

MAKES 2–4 SERVINGS

Start with a mound of sautéed garlic, add pasta, and you're already well on your way to crafting a foolproof dinner. Variations on the concept are as numerous as the creatures in the sea. Case in point, shrimp scampi was always a big hit in my household growing up, a real savory indulgence reserved for special occasions. Though I was much more interested in the buttery noodles than the seafood, even before becoming vegan, I still find myself craving those same comforting flavors in both good times and bad. Suggesting that cashews could take the place of shrimp may seem like an impossible stretch, but hear me out on this one. Visually convincing with their perfect half-moon shapes, it takes just one little trick to bring the texture up to speed. Boiling the nuts alongside the pasta softens them to a more toothsome, chewy consistency, while maintaining a neutral flavor to absorb every drop of that luxurious sauce. Round out the meal with a green salad or fold in a generous handful of green peas if you're concerned about meeting your daily recommended vegetable allowance.

Begin by cooking the pasta first so that it's ready to go at the same time as the sauce. Bring a large stockpot of water to a boil and add in the dry pasta and cashews together. Cook until the noodles are al dente; drain, reserving ½ cup of the starchy water. Do not rinse the noodles.

Meanwhile, heat the oil and butter together in a medium-sized skillet over medium heat. Sauté the shallot and garlic until fragrant and translucent, about 2 minutes. Stir in the miso paste and nutritional yeast, mashing and mixing until they dissolve smoothly into the sauce. Quickly deglaze the pan with the wine, simmering for about 2 minutes to soften the bite of the alcohol. Add the lemon juice and pepper next, cooking for a minute or two longer for the flavors to meld.

Transfer the cooked pasta and cashews into the skillet and toss to thoroughly coat with sauce. Add in a splash of the reserved pasta cooking water to loosen up the sauce, adjusting the consistency to taste. Stir in the parsley and capers (if using) and serve right away.

½ Pound Linguine, Spaghetti, or Fettuccine

1 Cup Raw Whole Cashews

1 Tablespoon Olive Oil

1 Tablespoon Vegan Butter

1 Medium Shallot, Finely Diced

4 Cloves Garlic, Minced

1 Tablespoon Chickpea or White Miso Paste

1 Tablespoon Nutritional Yeast

3 Tablespoons Dry White Wine or Vegetable Stock

3 Tablespoons Lemon Juice

¼ Teaspoon Ground Black Pepper

¼ Cup Fresh Parsley, Minced

1 Tablespoon Capers (Optional)

Lighten up! Ditch the pasta in favor of spiralized zucchini noodles, or keep it simple by plating the scampi over gently steamed spinach. Just boil the cashews by themselves for 6–8 minutes before adding them to the sauce.

Couscous Biryani

MAKES 4–6 SERVINGS

Biryani was once the fare of royalty, a feast for the eyes and the stomach that only the most affluent could afford. The golden mounds of tender grains glitter like a pile of shiny coins, interspersed with all manner of sweet and savory treasures. Bathed in a luxurious sauna of diverse spices, this illustrious one-pot wonder is now well within the grasp of anyone who has access to the average mega mart. Generous doses of protein and fiber allow this recipe to morph into either a main or a side, depending on your mood. Chicken biryani is the most popular variant, but aside from the obvious plant-based substitution, crispy tofu or cooked lentils make for other magnificent, if not downright kingly, additions.

Melt the coconut oil in a large saucepan over medium-high heat. Add the onion, ginger, garlic, and cumin seeds, sautéing for 3–4 minutes or until lightly browned. Mix in the remaining spices, stirring constantly, and cook over high heat for just 15–30 seconds. Add the water, followed by the carrots, tomato, raisins, peas, chickpeas, and salt.

Slowly sprinkle in the dry couscous while stirring to prevent it from clumping. Continue to cook, stirring periodically, until the water comes to a boil. Cover, reduce the heat to medium-low, and let simmer until liquid is absorbed. Uncover, remove from heat and let stand for at least 2 more minutes. Fluff couscous with a fork before transferring to a serving platter and topping with the cilantro and cashews.

Quick Tip: If your spice rack isn't quite so well stocked, trade in the cumin, garam masala, mustard seeds, turmeric, cinnamon, and cardamom for 3¼ teaspoons madras curry powder. The final flavor won't be nearly as nuanced, but the overall eating experience will be exactly as satisfying.

- 2 Tablespoons Coconut Oil
- ½ Cup (About ½ Small) Diced Yellow Onion
- 2 Teaspoon Grated Fresh Ginger
- 2 Cloves Garlic, Minced
- 1 Teaspoon Whole Cumin Seeds
- 1 Teaspoon Garam Masala
- ½ Teaspoon Whole Mustard Seeds
- ¼ Teaspoon Ground Turmeric
- ¼ Teaspoon Ground Cinnamon
- ⅛ Teaspoon Ground Cardamom
- 2 Cups Water
- ½ Cup Shredded Carrots
- ½ Cup (About 1 Medium) Diced Tomato
- ⅓ Cup Raisins
- ⅓ Cup Frozen Peas, Thawed
- 1 14-Ounce Can (1½ Cups Cooked) Chickpeas, Drained and Rinsed
- ½ Teaspoon Salt
- 1 Cup Couscous
- ½ Cup Chopped Fresh Cilantro
- ⅓ Cup Toasted Cashews

Daikon Scallop Skewers

MAKE 10–12 SKEWERS; 2–4 SERVINGS

"It's Top Chef, not Top Scallop!" Reality TV rarely spawns good ideas, but Top Chef is my guilty cooking competition indulgence. Every Thursday evening at 10:00 sharp, I'd plop down in front of the TV, laptop at hand, and stay glued to the spot as accomplished cooks raced to outdo one another. Seeing the contestants pull from unlikely sources of inspiration and diverse cultural backgrounds, by the time the hour had elapsed and another unfortunate soul had been told to pack their knives and go, my computer screen would be filled with new ideas to explore.

Scallops played prominently in one memorable season, so naturally, I found myself quite curious about their appeal. Daikon, woefully underappreciated by western cooks, has a lot to offer as a blank slate primed for embellishment. Tender and toothsome when cooked, beautifully seared over high heat, they play the lead role quite admirably. All they need is a bit of seasoning assistance in the form of kelp to impress a more oceanic essence. You could very happily skip the skewers for a more casual presentation, but to elevate the dish to Top Chef standards, that extra touch of finesse may just help sway the judges in your favor.

Soak 12–14 wooden or bamboo skewers in water, to prevent them from burning on the stove. Speed up the process by microwaving them on high, submerged in water, at full power for 30–60 seconds. If using metal skewers, simply proceed without delay.

Set a medium skillet over high heat and add in the oil. While that comes up to temperature, thread the daikon and asparagus onto your skewers, alternating the vegetables as desired. Toss them into the blisteringly-hot pan and don't touch them for the first 2 minutes to achieve a good sear.

While they cook, whisk together the vegetable stock, miso paste, lemon juice, garlic, kelp powder, and black pepper. Flip the skewers and cook for another 1–2 minutes, until evenly browned on both sides. Quickly pour in the liquid and prepare yourself for it to sizzle and sputter angrily—you might want to stand back! Turn down the heat to medium and let the mixture simmer for 3–5 minutes, turning the skewers once more if not entirely submerged in the stock, until the daikon pieces are tender and the excess liquid has evaporated.

Serve with a sprinkle of parsley over the top for a bit of extra flair.

1 Tablespoon Olive Oil

1 Medium (About 10 Inches Long; 8 Ounces) Daikon, Peeled and Sliced into ½-Inch Rounds

6–8 Fat Stalks (¼–½ Pound Total) Asparagus, Trimmed and Cut into 1-Inch Lengths

¼ Cup Vegetable Stock

1½ Tablespoons White Miso Paste

1 Tablespoon Lemon Juice

½ Teaspoon Garlic Powder

½ Teaspoon Kelp Powder

¼ Teaspoon Ground Black Pepper

Fresh Minced Parsley, to Taste

Quick Fix: Skip the skewers and serve this dish like a simple stir fry to slash prep time in half.

Enoki Ropa Vieja

MAKES 2–4 SERVINGS

Some recipes can start your mouth watering just from the title alone. A good food writer manipulates readers with descriptions carefully woven together that elicit nostalgia while simultaneously stirring up excitement over the promises of a new, novel eating experience. Ropa vieja is not like that. It translates directly as "old clothes," referring to the shredded texture of the dish. If you're expecting a mouthful of ratty cloth, though, you'll be happily surprised by the smoky umami bomb that meets your tongue instead. The long, spindly stems of tender enoki mushrooms stand in for overcooked strands of steak, both shortening the cooking time and opening up a brave new world of flavor. It can be enjoyed all by itself as a one-pot stew, on top of rice, alongside fried plantains, or with thick slices of crusty bread.

Heat the oil in a large saucepan over high heat. Begin sautéing the onion, red pepper, and garlic, stirring constantly to brown the edges without burning them. After about a minute, pull apart the enoki mushrooms in small clumps and add them to the pot. Turn the heat down slightly to medium-low and continue to cook, until the vegetables have softened and the mushrooms have expressed a bit of liquid.

Stir in the tomato paste, working it in vigorously to ensure that there are no clumps. Follow that with the soy sauce, liquid smoke, cumin, thyme, oregano, bay leaf, ⅓ cup of the vegetable stock, capers, and vinegar. Mix well to combine, and don't be afraid to get more aggressive if you need to break up the mushrooms more with your spatula. Bring up to a lively simmer and let cook for another 5–7 minutes, until the vegetables have all wilted down and become fork-tender. Add in the remaining stock if needed to prevent the mixture from sticking to the bottom of the pan, or if you prefer your dish on the saucier side.

Remove from the heat, top with fresh cilantro, and serve immediately.

- 1 Tablespoon Olive Oil
- ½ Medium Yellow Onion, Thinly Sliced
- 1 Red Bell Pepper, Seeded and Thinly Sliced
- 2 Cloves Garlic, Finely Minced
- 12 Ounces Enoki Mushrooms
- ¼ Cup Tomato Paste
- 1 Tablespoon Soy Sauce
- ½ Teaspoon Liquid Smoke
- 1½ Teaspoons Ground Cumin
- 1 Teaspoon Dried Thyme
- 1 Teaspoon Dried Oregano
- 1 Small Bay Leaf, Crumbled
- ⅓–½ Cups Vegetable Stock
- 1 Tablespoon Capers, Drained
- 1 Tablespoon Apple Cider Vinegar
- ¼ Cup Cilantro, Roughly Chopped

Jamaican Jerk Chili

MAKES 6–8 SERVINGS

Sound the alarm! It's hard to say where this Caribbean-inspired stew might rank in terms of pure Scoville units, but it definitely brings the heat. Unassuming little habaneros contribute the blistering blaze, turning up the heat with even the smallest addition. If you'd prefer a full-flavored blend that simply has a bit less fire power, feel free to omit the fresh pepper entirely. The unique Jamaican-style seasoning still packs a spicy, savory punch.

Set a large saucepan over medium-high heat and add the oil and crumbled tempeh. Sauté for a minute or two, until lightly browned, before adding in the minced habanero. Cook for a minute longer to release the volatile oils of the pepper that contain all its fiery flavor.

Simply incorporate all the remaining ingredients, starting with ½ teaspoon of the salt, and stir thoroughly to combine. Cover and bring to a full boil. Reduce the heat to medium and simmer for 3–6 minutes, stirring periodically, until slightly thickened and hot all the way through. Add the remaining salt to taste, if needed.

1 Tablespoon Olive Oil

8 Ounces Tempeh, Crumbled

½–1 Habanero Pepper, Seeded and Finely Minced

2 (14-Ounce) Cans Black-Eyed Peas

1 (14-Ounce) Can Fire-Roasted Diced Tomatoes

1 (6-Ounce) Can Tomato Paste

2 Tablespoons Molasses

2 Tablespoons Soy Sauce

1 Tablespoon Dehydrated Onion Flakes

1 Tablespoon Garlic Powder

2 Teaspoons Dried Thyme

1 Teaspoon Ground Allspice

1 Teaspoon Hot Paprika

¾ Teaspoon Ground Black Pepper

½ Teaspoon Cayenne Pepper

½ Teaspoon Crushed Red Pepper Flakes

¼ Teaspoon Ground Cumin

¼ Teaspoon Ground Cinnamon

½–¾ Teaspoon Salt

Quick Tip: Don't have a particularly well-stocked spice rack? Grab a bottle of Jamaican jerk seasoning blend and use 3 tablespoons of the mix instead of the individual spices called for, from the onion flakes straight through to the salt.

Laab

MAKES 3–4 SERVINGS

Laap, laab, larp, lahb, larb; no matter how you spell it (or say it), this winning minced meat salad is regarded by many as the national dish of Laos. No one country can contain its delicious potential though, which is why you'll often find variations on the theme pop up on Thai, Burmese, and Chinese menus as well. Tender lettuce cups cradle mounds of highly flavorful protein, flecked with herbs and peppery spices. Though simple in concept and preparation, the finished combination, both cooling and boldly invigorating at once, proves why it's taken hold in so many diverse cultures. If you like it especially hot, there's no shame in dressing each fiery bite with additional sriracha to taste.

Set a dry medium skillet over moderate heat and begin by toasting the rice flour by itself. Give it about a minute to take on a light golden color, shaking the pan constantly to ensure even browning. Transfer to a separate dish and set aside.

Return the skillet to the stove but increase the heat to medium-high. Add both oils, garlic, ginger, onion, and mushrooms, and sauté for 2–3 minutes. The onions should have softened and the entire mixture will be highly aromatic. Introduce your meatless crumbles of choice next, stirring gently so as not to break up the clumps too much. Sauté until nicely browned all over, about 4–5 minutes.

Deglaze the pan with the lime juice and liquid aminos, using your spatula to scrape up all the delicious caramelized vegetables at the bottom. Follow that with the sugar and crushed red pepper, stirring to incorporate. Allow the mixture to cook just until the liquid has absorbed into the meaty matrix. Turn off the heat, fold in the scallions, mint, and toasted rice powder. Transfer to a serving dish and let guests assemble their own leafy wraps, completing the assembly with a sprinkle of chopped peanuts.

LAAB:

- 1 Tablespoon White Rice Flour
- 1 Teaspoon Sesame Oil
- 2 Tablespoons Olive Oil
- 2 Cloves Garlic, Minced
- 1 Tablespoon Minced Fresh Ginger
- ⅓ Cup Minced Red Onion
- 5 Fresh Shiitake Mushroom Caps, Finely Diced
- 12 Ounces Crumbled Tempeh or Meatless Beef-Style Crumbles
- 2 Tablespoons Lime Juice
- 1 Tablespoon Bragg Liquid Aminos
- 1 Tablespoon Coconut Sugar or Light Brown Sugar, Firmly Packed
- ½–1 Teaspoon Crushed Red Pepper Flakes
- 2 Scallions, Thinly Sliced
- 2 Tablespoons Roughly Chopped Fresh Mint

TO SERVE:

- 1 Head Savoy Cabbage or Butter Lettuce, Leaves Separated
- ¼ Cup Finely Chopped Roasted Peanuts

Mofongo Bowls

MAKES 2–4 SERVINGS

Mofongo is no beauty queen, but beneath that starchy exterior lies a heart of gold. Green plantains mashed with garlic and adobo seasoning are so delicious that they're often eaten straight out of the mortar and pestle, filled or topped with any combination of seafood, meat, or vegetables. Vegetarian versions are admittedly hard to come by in Puerto Rican kitchens, but mojo marinade, a zesty mélange of herbs and citrus, covers anything with an equal appeal. Either component could be served as a highly successful side dish, but they are greater than the sum of their parts when joined together in this one-bowl wonder.

Plantains are much like tropical potatoes in the sense that they must be cooked through for the starchy flesh to soften and become edible. Peel the plantains and place them in a microwave-safe dish with just enough vegetable stock to cover. Heat on full power for 3–5 minutes, checking them every 90 seconds or so, until fork-tender.

Meanwhile, sauté the garlic in the olive oil in a skillet over medium heat. When lightly golden brown, stir in the adobo seasoning, and add everything to the cooked plantains. Roughly mash with a potato masher, slowly adding the remaining stock until creamy, leaving the texture slightly chunky. Keep warm.

For the black beans, simply toss all the ingredients together in a large bowl to combine and evenly coat the beans. Add salt to taste. This can be served right away, at room temperature or heated over the medium-low on the stove or microwave for 1–2 minutes, just until warm.

Smooth equal portions of the mashed plantains into the bottoms of large bowls and top with the seasoned black beans. Finish with an extra pinch of fresh cilantro, if desired.

> *DIY, don't buy! Adobo seasoning is made simply with equal parts salt, hot paprika, ground black pepper, dried oregano, ground cumin, onion powder, garlic powder, and chili powder.

MASHED PLANTAINS:

- 1½ Pounds (About 2 Large) Green Plantains
- 1–1½ Cups Vegetable Stock
- 2 Cloves Garlic, Minced
- 2 Tablespoons Olive Oil
- 1 Teaspoon Adobo Seasoning*

MOJO BLACK BEANS:

- 2 Tablespoons Olive Oil
- ½ Cup Fresh Cilantro, Roughly Chopped
- 1 Teaspoon Finely Grated Orange Zest
- 2 Tablespoons Orange Juice
- 2 Tablespoons Lime Juice
- 1 Tablespoon Fresh Mint, Roughly Chopped
- 2 Cloves Garlic, Minced
- ½ Teaspoon Dried Oregano
- ¾ Teaspoon Ground Cumin
- ½–1 Teaspoon Salt
- 1 14-Ounce Can (or 1½ Cups Cooked) Black Beans, Rinsed and Drained

Palak Paneer Panini

MAKES 3 SERVINGS

Leftovers are a big selling point when dining out or ordering in. Flavorful curries take on unparalleled complexity after a night in the fridge, mingling and balancing each other out like a group of close-knit friends. Harsh edges mellow while more subtle accents come to the fore. It doesn't take much to jazz up the excess for round two, which is what led to this unconventional sandwich inspiration. Stewed spinach and cheese-like tofu curds sparkle with cumin and garam masala, pressed between two crisp slices of crusty bread. There's no need to wait for the doggy bag when that same combination can be whipped up from scratch in the comfort of your own kitchen.

Melt 1 tablespoon of the coconut oil in a large saucepan over medium heat. Add in the garlic and onion, sautéing for 2–3 minutes until translucent. Toss in the cumin and garam masala, mixing the spices in and allowing them to toast for about a minute. You want to coax out their full flavor potential with a bit of direct heat, but be careful to keep stirring constantly to prevent them from burning.

Add the spinach, a few handfuls at a time, folding it in until it wilts down and all fits comfortably into the pan. This should happen very quickly; as soon as the greens are tender and vibrant, take the pan off the heat. Cool things down with the yogurt or sour cream, and follow that with the lemon zest, salt, and sun-dried tomato. Stir everything in thoroughly.

To assemble the sandwiches, take a clean skillet or grill pan and set it over medium-high heat. Stuff your bread of choice with equal portions of the seasoned spinach, layering the tofu "paneer" slices in the center. Spread the outsides of the sandwiches with the remaining coconut oil and move them into the pan. Apply firm but gentle pressure with your spatula, compressing each panini. Cook for 2 minutes, until toasted and golden brown, before flipping. Repeat on opposite side.

Slice the sandwiches in half or just chow down as soon as the sandwiches come off the grill.

Ingredients:

- 3 Tablespoons Coconut Oil, Divided
- 2 Cloves Garlic, Minced
- 2 Tablespoons Diced Yellow Onion
- ½ Teaspoon Whole Cumin Seeds
- 1 Teaspoon Garam Masala
- 5–6 Ounces (About 4 Cups Lightly Packed) Baby Spinach
- 2 Tablespoons Plain, Unsweetened Vegan Yogurt or Sour Cream
- ½ Teaspoon Lemon Zest
- ½ Teaspoon Salt
- ¼ Cup Sliced Sun-Dried Tomatoes
- 3 (4-Ounce) Ciabatta Rolls, Dutch-Crunch Rolls, or 6 Slices Sandwich Bread
- 7 Ounces Extra-Firm Tofu, Cut Lengthwise into ½-Inch Slabs

Eat your greens! Add variety to your diet and swap the spinach for kale, watercress, or mustard greens to spread the leafy love around.

Pizza Waffles

MAKES ABOUT 12 WAFFLES; 4-6 SERVINGS

While the adage that breakfast is the most important meal of the day is hotly contested, there's no argument that breakfast foods are among the most popular. At any diner worth its salt, breakfast options outnumber those for lunch and dinner combined. Those same eateries know that breakfast shouldn't be confined to only AM hours. Thus, when waffles meet pizza in a timeless entree, it's a beautiful evolution to behold. Chickpea flour adds a subtly nutty flavor and extra protein to the hearty base, crispy right out of the iron and primed for your favorite toppings. Thinly sliced onions, olives, roasted red peppers, artichokes, mushrooms, and yes, pineapple if you're into that. Pile on your picks like mini pizzas, or enjoy them plain with sauce on the side for your dipping pleasure!

Begin preheating your waffle iron straightaway so that it will be hot and ready to go as soon as your batter is ready.

In a large bowl, whisk together both flours, nutritional yeast, all the herbs and spices, baking powder and soda, and salt. Stir thoroughly to ensure that all the dry goods are equally distributed.

Separately, whisk together the nondairy milk, pizza sauce, and oil. Pour the liquid mixture into the large bowl of dry, and use a wide spatula to combine the two, stirring just until the batter is smooth. A few errant lumps are fine to leave behind, lest you over-mix and end up with tough waffles.

Lightly grease the waiting waffle iron and dole out about ⅓–½ cup batter for each waffle pizza. Clamp the lid shut and let it cook on medium to medium-high heat for 3–6 minutes, depending on your machine. Once golden brown and crisp on the outside, pull the waffles out onto a plate and dress up with any accoutrement your heart desires. The waffles can also be made in advance and stored in the fridge for up to three days, or in the freezer for up to three months.

Quick Tip: Short on specific spices? Substitute 2 tablespoons Italian seasoning for the dried oregano, dried basil, garlic powder, dried thyme, and crushed red pepper flakes.

Quick Tip: Want a more "authentic" pizza parlor experience? Use prepared, refrigerated pizza dough instead. Tear off tennis ball-sized pieces, roll them into rounds, and press them into the waffle iron.

PIZZA WAFFLES:

1 Cup Garbanzo Bean Flour

1 Cup All-Purpose Flour

2 Tablespoons Nutritional Yeast

2 Teaspoons Dehydrated Onion Flakes

2 Teaspoons Dried Oregano

2 Teaspoons Dried Basil

1 Teaspoon Garlic Powder

½ Teaspoon Dried Thyme

½ Teaspoon Crushed Red Pepper Flakes

2 Teaspoons Baking Powder

½ Teaspoon Baking Soda

½ Teaspoon Salt

1½ Cups Unsweetened Nondairy Milk

⅔ Cup Pizza Sauce

6 Tablespoons Olive Oil

TO SERVE:

Additional Pizza Sauce

Nutritional Yeast or Shredded Vegan Cheese

Toppings (See Above for Suggestions, or Choose Your Own Adventure)

Sausage Gumbo Burgers

Makes 4 Servings

For a dish that's synonymous with The Big Easy, gumbo is a quite a complicated ordeal. Starting with the roux, a hotly debated yet essential Creole compound, you could write a novel about the merits of using various types of flour, how light or dark it should be when cooked, and if it should be the sole thickener of the stew. That's before we even begin discussing the meat of the matter! Sausage is widely accepted as the gold standard at least, which is what inspired this handheld reinterpretation of the low country classic. The savory patties could be eaten as a stand-alone breakfast staple, but when dressed up with all the fixings of a hearty okra gumbo, you'll never want to waste time cooking it the old-fashioned away again. Let the good times roll and get this crowd-pleaser on the table before the band starts to play!

In a large bowl, coarsely mash the red beans and fold in the minced celery. Add the tomato paste, soy sauce, tahini or peanut butter, sugar, and liquid smoke, stirring to incorporate. Separately, whisk together the wheat gluten, garlic powder, paprika, thyme, oregano, basil, black pepper, fennel seeds, and cayenne. Stir until all the dry goods are thoroughly combined before adding the mixture into the bowl of wet ingredients. Use a wide spatula to fold everything together, getting your hands in there if need be, to make sure there are no remaining pockets of dry ingredients. If the dough is still especially sticky, add in an extra tablespoon or so of wheat gluten, but it should remain somewhat soft.

Place a large skillet over medium heat and add the oil. Meanwhile, divide the savory dough into four equal pieces and shape them into smooth rounds between lightly moistened palms. Place them into the hot pan, pressing them down to flatten each one into approximately ½-inch thick patties. Fry for 3–5 minutes on each side, flipping when golden brown all over.

Serve on hamburger buns with strips of roasted red pepper, pickled okra, sliced onions, and hot sauce, if desired.

Sausage-Spiced Patties:

- 1 Cup Cooked Red Beans
- ¼ Cup Finely Minced Celery
- 3 Tablespoons Tomato Paste
- 2 Tablespoons Soy Sauce
- 1 Tablespoon Tahini or Smooth Peanut Butter
- 1 Teaspoon Dark Brown Sugar, Firmly Packed
- ½ Teaspoon Liquid Smoke
- ½ Cup Vital Wheat Gluten
- 1 Teaspoon Garlic Powder
- 1 Teaspoon Smoked Paprika
- ½ Teaspoon Dried Thyme
- ½ Teaspoon Dried Oregano
- ½ Teaspoon Dried Basil
- ¼ Teaspoon Ground Black Pepper
- ¼ Teaspoon Whole Fennel Seeds
- ⅛ Teaspoon Cayenne Pepper
- 1 Tablespoon Olive Oil

Continued on page 186

To Assemble:

4 Burger Buns
Roasted Red Peppers
Pickled Okra*
Thinly Sliced Red Onions
Hot Sauce (Optional)

*Pickled okra can be found in most grocery stores and specialty markets this days, typically amongst the shelf-stable pickles and canned vegetables, but you can also whip up your own in just a few minutes. This is best when okra is in season and impeccably fresh. If you can plan ahead, these only get better with age. Alternatively, you could simply toss some fresh okra on the grill, give it a nice char, and call it a day.

Quick Pickled Okra:

½ Pound Okra, Sliced into 1-Inch Pieces
1 Cup White Vinegar or Apple Cider Vinegar
1 Cup Water
2 Tablespoons Sugar
1 Tablespoon Salt
2 Teaspoons Whole Coriander Seeds, Roughly Crushed

Place the cut okra in a pint jar and set aside.

Combine the vinegar, water, sugar, salt, and coriander seeds in a medium saucepan over moderate heat. Bring to a boil, stir to dissolve the sugar and salt. Immediately pour the hot liquid into the jar, over the okra. Let stand for at least 10 minutes before serving, and refrigerate for up to two weeks if not enjoying right away.

Rinse under cold water before using to cut down on the slime.

Makes 1 Pint

Seitan Bulgogi

MAKES 4–5 SERVINGS

Sizzling violently upon a cast iron platter, the best bulgogi is an all-out assault on the senses. It speaks loudly, crackling and radiating with heat, taking on an eerily lifelike quality as steam envelops the dish. Pungent, breathing fiery aroma from a mile away, you'll know it's coming long before it hits the table. This arresting experience is typically the result of hours of marinating, but slicing seitan very thin allows you to accelerate through the prep work and cut right to the show. Bring the fire to sear the "meat" over the hottest flame you can tolerate without burning down the house, and your risk will be rewarded tenfold. The crispy bits around the edges are the best parts, which will be in no shortage thanks to the extreme heat and blazingly fast cook time.

Create the marinade by simply tossing the pear, garlic, ginger, soy sauce, vinegar, and pepper flakes into your blender and thoroughly pureeing. Pause to scrape down the sides of the container if needed to combine all the ingredients. It's perfectly fine if it's not entirely smooth, since a bit of texture won't hurt here. You just want a well-combined sauce that can coat the seitan nicely.

Meanwhile, set a large cast iron pan or skillet on the stove and crank up the heat to high. Add in the oil and wait for it to shimmer, getting it very hot but just shy of smoking. Introduce the plain seitan first, mixing slowly but constantly, flipping the pieces to make sure they all get an equal amount of time in full contact with the bottom of the pan. Sauté until nicely browned all over; 3–4 minutes.

Smother the seitan with the blended sauce, pouring the mixture into the pan in one big sizzling addition, tossing to completely coat all the pieces. Be sure to scrape the sides and bottom of the pan as it sears to prevent anything from sticking and burning. Continue to cook for about 4–5 minutes, until highly aromatic and crispy around the edges.

Transfer to a serving platter, top with scallions, and serve over rice, in lettuce wraps, or alongside sliced cucumbers.

1 Ripe Pear, Peeled, Cored, and Diced

2 Cloves Garlic, Finely Minced

1 Tablespoon Minced Fresh Ginger

¼ Cup Soy Sauce

1 Tablespoon Rice Vinegar

2 Teaspoons Gochugaru (Korean Hot Pepper Flakes) or 1–1½ Teaspoons Crushed Red Pepper Flakes

1 Tablespoon Toasted Sesame Oil

1 Pound Seitan, Thinly Sliced

3 Scallions, Thinly Sliced

Sloppy Jacks

MAKES 3–4 SERVINGS

Quite frankly, I don't know jack about Sloppy Joes. I didn't grow up eating them and was utterly clueless about the concept well into my mid-twenties. Happily, the comforting tomato-based sandwich is not an acquired taste, gained only from a lifetime of experience but one of broad, automatic appeal. Rather than spoil Joe with all the attention though, I'm happy to share the love with Jack—jackfruit, that is. Standing in for shredded "meat," it lends a more substantial bite to the assembly without straying too far from its humble origins. True to form, the eating experience can get very sloppy, very fast, and I mark that as a genuine success.

Heat the oil in a large skillet or medium saucepan over medium-high heat and toss in the onion and bell pepper. Sauté until the vegetables are softened, aromatic, and just beginning to take on a bit of brown color around the edges; about 2–3 minutes. Sprinkle in the chili and garlic powder, stirring well to combine and cooking for just a few seconds to allow the flavors to mingle.

Introduce the jackfruit next, sautéing for about a minute before following it with the tomato paste, water, sugar, mustard, vinegar, and soy sauce. Stir well to incorporate, thoroughly coating the jackfruit and using your spatula or a potato masher to break it up into finer threads. Don't be afraid to get aggressive; get in there and smash it roughly until the consistency is to your liking.

Drop the heat down to medium or medium-low, and simmer until some of the liquid has evaporated and the sauce clings thickly to the jackfruit. Stir periodically for about 4–5 minutes, depending on the power of your stove. Season with salt and pepper to taste.

Serve hot, on your bread of choice with a handful of crisp cabbage or lettuce.

SLOPPY JACKFRUIT:

- 1 Tablespoon Olive Oil
- 1 Medium Yellow Onion, Diced
- ½ Green Bell Pepper, Seeded and Diced
- 1 Teaspoon Chili Powder
- 1 Teaspoon Garlic Powder
- 1 (10.6 Ounce Shelf-Stable Package) Jackfruit or 1 20-Ounce Can Young Jackfruit in Brine, Drained
- ¾ Cup (6 Ounces) Tomato Paste
- 1–3 Tablespoons Water
- 2 Teaspoons Dark Brown Sugar, Firmly Packed
- 1 Teaspoon Dijon Mustard
- 1 Teaspoon Apple Cider Vinegar
- 1 Tablespoon Soy Sauce
- ¼–½ Teaspoon Salt
- ¼ Teaspoon Ground Black Pepper

TO SERVE:

- 3–4 Soft Sandwich Buns or Kaiser Rolls
- Finely Shredded Cabbage or Lettuce

Tamale Pot Pies

Diving head-first into veganism as an unseasoned adolescent, I had zero culinary skills to speak of when I abruptly found myself alone in the kitchen. That frequently meant rubbery tofu pups skewered and "grilled" over an open stovetop burner, or waxy slices of Day-Glo orange "cheese" warmed between slices of dry whole wheat bread. Far from an auspicious start to a passionate career in food, I would have likely starved in those early years if not for a few merciful frozen meals. Tamale pies, individual cardboard bowls filled with mildly spiced beans and vegetables, topped off with a thin sheet of soft polenta, were my saving grace in high school. Many years later, I've found it takes little more effort to whip up the whole dish from scratch, taking a shortcut on the polenta by simply slicing off tender rounds from a readymade tube. In particularly busy times, the pies can be assembled in advance, frozen, and reheated whenever hunger strikes.

Have four 10-ounce ramekins or one 1-quart casserole dish at the ready.

Set a medium-sized skillet over medium-high heat and add 1 tablespoon of the oil. Once hot, toss in the onion and garlic, sautéing for about 2–3 minutes until aromatic and lightly golden. Stir in the all the spices, herbs, and salt, cooking for just a minute longer to release their essential flavors and heat through.

Add the beans, corn, salsa, and tomato paste, taking care to work out any lumps of tomato paste before proceeding. Let the whole stew simmer gently for 5 minutes to meld the flavors before taking the pan off the heat. Spoon the filling into your prepared ramekins, doling out equal amounts to each, or spread it all evenly into a casserole dish. Top with slices of the prepared polenta (you will likely have more than you need; you can either double up to fully cover the entire surface, cutting them further to fit, or save the remainder for another recipe), brush with the remaining olive oil, and run them under the broiler, just until lightly golden.

Finish with a light sprinkle of cilantro, if desired, and serve piping hot!

2 Tablespoons Olive Oil, Divided

½ Cup Diced (About ½ Medium) Red Onion

1 Clove Garlic, Minced

1½ Teaspoons Chili Powder

1 Teaspoon Ground Cumin

½ Teaspoon Dried Oregano

½ Teaspoon Salt

1 14-Ounce Can (1½ Cups Cooked) Black Beans

1 Cup Corn Kernels, Canned and Drained or Frozen and Thawed

2 Cups Chunky Salsa, Excess Liquid Drained

¼ Cup Tomato Paste

1 (16-Ounce) Tube Prepared Polenta, Cut into ½-Inch Slices

Fresh Cilantro (Optional)

Quick Fix: Multitask to save time and get crispier edges on your polenta. Place the slices on a lightly greased sheet pan, brush with oil, and slide them under the broiler right away, before starting the rest of the stew. By the time the filling is hot and ready, your polenta rounds will be beautifully burnished golden brown. Just move them on top of the ramekins and they're good to go!

Walnut Bolognese

MAKES 3–4 SERVINGS

Calling upon walnuts to take the place of beef in this classic red sauce is only common sense; the edible kernel found within those hard shells is formally known as "nutmeat" to begin with, so it's not as great a chasm to bridge as it may first seem. When cooked, the crumbles soften and tenderize with surprising ease, revealing their true meaty nature. Prepared marinara makes an instant base to build upon, enhanced by the natural and subtle sweetness of shredded carrots in concert with a battery of herbs and spices. The beauty of the dish lies in its utter simplicity, completely satisfying in its most basic form, but easily enhanced with any extra vegetables you might have kicking around in the fridge. For a particularly power-hungry crowd, boost the protein quotient by throwing in a handful of hemp seeds or cooked lentils, too.

Set a large skillet over high heat and add in the oil. Once hot, begin to sauté the onion, garlic, and carrots, cooking for 2–3 minutes. Stir constantly to prevent excessive browning or burning. Add the marinara, along with the soy sauce, dried basil, and red pepper flakes, stirring to incorporate. Bring the mixture up to a lively simmer. Cook for 3–4 minutes to allow the flavors to meld. Add the chopped walnuts last, cooking for just 1 minute longer. Toss the cooked noodles with sauce and serve immediately.

2 Tablespoons Olive Oil

½ Medium Yellow Onion, Diced

3 Cloves Garlic, Minced

1 Cup Shredded Carrots

2 Cups Marinara Sauce

1 Tablespoon Soy Sauce

1 Teaspoon Dried Basil

¼ Teaspoon Crushed Red Pepper Flakes

1½ Cups Raw Walnuts, Roughly Chopped

TO SERVE:

¾ Pound Linguine, Fettuccine, or Spaghetti, Cooked

Effortlessly add variety to the menu by trying a new type of marinara. Opt for a chunkier sauce to lend more texture to your ragout, and look for one that includes mushrooms to add an extra meaty element.

DESSERTS AND SWEETS

Black Forest Skillet Crisp

MAKES 4–8 SERVINGS

Tearing through the orchard like a puppy unleashed, my face stained red with sweet cherry juices, I must have eaten as many cherries as I collected on my first u-pick experience. That's saying something, because I still went home with a bounty of fresh fruit weighing in excess of six pounds. Though it would have been no struggle to keep on plowing through the pile unadorned, the possibilities for enhancement were even more irresistible.

Warm fruit crisp straight out of the oven, still bubbling richly with gooey baked fruit, is a truly underrated pleasure. This version skips the preheating and baking time, cooked straight over the stove instead. Chocolate mingles with explosively ripe cherries for all the flavor of Black Forest cake, with none of the hassle.

Starting with the streusel, combine the flour, almond meal, rolled oats, sugar, salt, and cinnamon in a medium-sized bowl. Drizzle in the melted butter or coconut oil, stirring until large clumps form and the entire mixture is moistened. Transfer to a small skillet and cook on low heat, stirring frequently, until the streusel is golden brown and well toasted, 6–8 minutes. (The streusel can also be made up to a week in advance. After cooling completely, store in an airtight container at room temperature until ready to use.)

Meanwhile, for the filling, place the cherries in a large skillet and begin to cook over medium heat. Mix together the sugar, cocoa powder, and cornstarch in a small bowl before adding it to the fruit. Stir thoroughly to incorporate and heat until the natural juices of the cherries come up to a simmer. Stir periodically, until the cherries have burst and the surrounding liquid has thickened, about 8–9 minutes. Mix in the almond extract and salt last.

Top with the streusel and serve immediately, right out of the skillet.

Quick Tip: Skip the streusel and throw 1½ cups of your favorite granola on top instead. Toss it with a few tablespoons of melted vegan butter or coconut oil to make it a bit richer.

STREUSEL:

½ Cup All-Purpose Flour

½ Cup Blanched Almond Meal

½ Cup Old-Fashioned Rolled Oats

½ Cup Light Brown Sugar, Firmly Packed

½ Teaspoon Salt

½ Teaspoon Ground Cinnamon

½ Cup Vegan Butter or Coconut Oil, Melted

CHOCOLATE-CHERRY FILLING:

2 Pounds (About 4 Cups) Frozen Pitted Sweet Cherries, Thawed

⅓ Cup Granulated Sugar

3 Tablespoons Cocoa Powder

2 Tablespoons Cornstarch

½ Teaspoon Almond Extract

¼ Teaspoon Salt

Should you find yourself with an overabundance of fresh cherries after similar picking expeditions, you can save yourself time by pitting them in advance and freezing them on a single layer on a baking sheet. Store in ziplock bags in 1-pound portions for easy access.

Cashew Milkshakes

MAKES 1 SERVING

When the clock strikes midnight and I crave a sweet late-night fix, I turn not to the cookie jar nor candy dish, but to the freezer. Ice cream holds a special place in my heart; I could easily plow through a pint no matter the season, from the dog days of summer to the depths of a frigid winter. Milkshakes are the ultimate expressions of ice cream glory, soft enough to slurp through a straw, and just warm enough that all the flavors can fully express themselves while keeping their cool. The trouble is that I have a hard time keeping my spoon out of the container, leaving little if any left over for other applications. After many unfulfilled frustrations, some kitchen experimentation revealed that the creamiest, richest milkshakes don't need any ice cream at all. Raw cashews and ice cubes join forces in this impossibly thick and decadent drink, ready to dress up with your favorite flavors in an instant. Other neutral nuts can work in a pinch as well, such as blanched almonds or macadamia nuts. I daresay the results are even better than the conventional approach without making any compromises on effort or ingredients.

Bring the water (at least 1 cup, but the exact measure isn't critical) to a boil in a small saucepan over high heat and drop in the cashews. Cook at a rapid boil until the nuts are softened; about 5 minutes. Drain and plunge into ice-cold water. Drain thoroughly once more.

Transfer the nuts to your blender and puree, along with the cold water and sugar, on high speed for 3 minutes until smooth. Pause to scrape down the sides of the canister with your spatula as needed. Add in the vanilla, salt, and ice. Blend again until the mixture is completely creamy and silky smooth.

Serve immediately in a tall glass and, ideally, with a wide straw.

½ Cup Raw Cashew Pieces

Boiling Water, to Cover

½ Cup Cold Water

¼ Cup Coconut Sugar or Date Sugar

1 Teaspoon Vanilla Paste or Extract

⅛ Teaspoon Salt

8 Ice Cubes (About 1 Cup)

Choose your own flavor adventure! I adore the classic vanilla, but here are a few of my other top picks:

Matcha Mint Chip: Add 1 Teaspoon Matcha Powder, ½ Teaspoon Peppermint Extract, 2 Tablespoons Cacao Nibs or Finely Chopped Dark Chocolate

Chocolate: Add ¼ Cup Dutch-Processed Cocoa Powder

Strawberry: Add ¼ Cup Seedless Strawberry Jam and omit the sugar

Cheesecake-Stuffed Strawberries

MAKES 4–6 SERVINGS

As Valentine's Day approaches, love is in the air—along with a certain degree of panic. No matter how predictably it falls on February 14th, it always seems to sneak up on us. Even the most prepared love-struck partners struggle to meet the deadline, as the daily grind often distracts us at the most inopportune times.

Rekindle genuine romance at the drop of a hat by pulling this sweet shortcut out of your sleeve. Far better than flowers or store-bought chocolates, nothing shows your love better than a homemade gift. Sure, simple chocolate-covered strawberries are nice enough, but by going the extra mile and filling them to the brim with creamy cheesecake custard, you've made a truly memorable treat.

For starters, be sure to select large, plump strawberries to ensure a good ratio of fruit to cheesecake to chocolate in every bite. Wash and very thoroughly dry the strawberries. Use a sharp paring knife to slice off the stem and attached leaves on each strawberry. Carve out the center carefully, removing the core and a little bit around it to accommodate the filling. Set aside.

Beat together the cream cheese, confectioner's sugar, vanilla, and zest with an electric mixer or a sturdy spatula until completely smooth. Transfer the cheesecake mixture to a pastry bag or a ziplock bag with the corner snipped off, and carefully pipe the filling into your prepared, hollowed out berries. Mound it slightly over the top of each strawberry for the most visual impact.

Once all strawberries are filled, set out a sheet of waxed paper nearby and begin preparing the chocolate coating. Combine the chocolate chips and coconut oil in a microwave-safe dish and heat for 30–60 seconds, pausing to stir at the halfway point. Once fully melted and perfectly smooth, gently dip half of each strawberry into the liquid chocolate. Allow the excess coating to drip off before carefully placing the chocolate-covered berry on the wax paper. Repeat until all the berries are covered similarly, and let the chocolate set up in a cool place. Sprinkle the graham cracker crumbs lightly over the cream cheese mixture to finish.

Refrigerate berries until ready to serve; best if served within six hours.

Ingredients

- 1 Pound Fresh Strawberries
- 1 (8-Ounce) Package Vegan Cream Cheese
- ¼ Cup Confectioner's Sugar
- ½ Teaspoon Vanilla Paste or Extract
- ½ Teaspoon Lemon Zest
- 6 Ounces (1 Cup) Dark Chocolate Chips
- ½ Teaspoon Coconut Oil
- 2–3 Tablespoons Graham Cracker Crumbs

Quick Tip: Put down the piping bag and breeze through the assembly in half the time. Simply slice the strawberries in half, drop a dollop of the cheesecake filling on top, sprinkle with graham crackers, and drizzle with chocolate. For a quicker fix, just throw some miniature chocolate chips or roughly chopped chocolate pieces in with the graham cracker crumbs.

Grilled Bananas Foster Kebabs

MAKES 4 SERVINGS

Flame on! Playing with fire makes for a brilliant show, but the art of the flambé is a difficult one to master, if not downright dangerous. Pouring generous splashes of high-proof alcohol over an open flame just sounds like a recipe for disaster. Taking advantage of the grill's more controlled burn, skewered bananas take on an attractive char before plunging into a waiting pool of rum-spiked caramel sauce. These warm, fruity kebabs will practically melt in your mouth, without melting down your kitchen.

Begin by heating your grill, or a grill pan over the highest setting on your stove.

When cutting your bananas into coins, make sure they're thick enough that they won't split when skewered. Use either thin metal skewers or wooden skewers that have been soaked in water. This is to ensure that the more flammable wood doesn't ignite over the grill. Gently toss the cut bananas in orange juice first to prevent oxidization before threading them onto the skewers. Brush evenly with oil and toss them on the grill. Cook for 2–4 minutes on each side, until deeply charred in nice, consistent lines.

Meanwhile, melt the butter in a small saucepan over moderate heat. Add the brown sugar and cook until dissolved. Whisk together the rum, cornstarch, and salt separately before pouring the mixture into the pan. Whisk thoroughly to incorporate, simmering for 3–6 minutes until the sauce has thickened to a syrupy consistency. Turn off the heat before stirring in the orange zest.

Transfer the sauce to a small dish and dip to your heart's content. This combination is also delicious paired with ice cream, pound cake, granola . . . or all three!

GRILLED BANANA KEBABS:

4 Firm but Ripe Bananas, Sliced into Approximately 1-Inch Pieces

1 Tablespoon Orange Juice

1 Tablespoon Olive Oil

SPICED RUM CARAMEL DIP:

¼ Cup Vegan Butter

½ Cup Dark Brown Sugar

¼ Cup Dark Rum*

1 Teaspoon Cornstarch

½ Teaspoon Cinnamon

⅛ Teaspoon Salt

½ Teaspoon Finely Grated Orange Zest

*For a more kid-friendly treat, swap out the rum for orange juice.

Quick Tip: The caramel sauce can be prepared in advance and simply warmed for 30–60 seconds in the microwave when needed. Store it in an airtight container in the fridge for up to two weeks.

Mango Crème Brûlée

MAKES 4 SERVINGS

A crisp caramelized sugar topping elevates the average pudding to a whole new level, perfect for a fancy dinner party, elegant brunch, or just any day that a special treat is in order. Straddling that fine line between healthy and indulgent, the bright mango custard is merely blended until smooth, without added starches or other thickeners. Rich, but still healthy enough that you can feel good about getting a second helping.

Toss the mango, agave, ginger, and vanilla into your blender or food processor. Puree on high speed until completely smooth. Slowly stream in the melted coconut oil while continuing to blend. Divide the mixture equally between four 4-ounce ramekins. Place them in the freezer for about 5 minutes, just to keep the custard nice and cold.

Only prepare the brûlée topping right before serving. Sprinkle 1 teaspoon of the sugar over the top of each ramekin, evenly blanketing the entire surface. Use a kitchen torch or place the ramekins under a hot broiler set to high, and cook until the sugar turns golden brown, bubbles all over, and caramelizes. Serve immediately.

1½ Cups (About 1 Large) Cubed Ripe Mango

2 Tablespoons Light Agave Nectar

1 Teaspoon Minced Fresh Ginger

1 Teaspoon Vanilla Extract

¼ Cup Coconut Oil, Melted

4 Teaspoons Granulated Sugar

Quick Fix: Reach for frozen mango to skip the slippery task of cubing the fresh fruit.

Not in the mood for mango? Reach for any other sort of fleshy fruits, such as peaches, apricots, bananas, or berries—and don't be afraid to experiment with different combinations, too!

Peppermint Bark Meltaways

MAKES 16–20 CHOCOLATES

Imagine the richest, densest square of dark chocolate fudge, melting luxuriously the moment it hits your tongue, and you'd come close to the sheer decadence that is a chocolate meltaway. Adding coconut oil to pure chocolate lowers the melting point well below body temperature, creating a veritable tidal wave of liquid cacao with every bite. Best of all, it's far easier than the laborious stirring required for traditional fudge; just heat, stir, and set. You'll be in chocoholic heaven in minutes.

Peppermint extract and crushed candy canes give my twist on the concept a refreshingly bold blast of peppermint, much like you'd get with peppermint bark. They're perfect for holiday gifts, but can be a sweet breath of fresh air during the sweltering heat of summer, too.

Place the chocolate chips and coconut oil in a microwave-safe container and heat for 30–90 seconds, stirring at every 30-second interval, until completely melted and smooth. Mix in the peppermint extract and salt.

Pour the liquid chocolate into silicon ice cube or candy molds of any shape your heart desires (literally, as pictured!) or alternatively, use an 8x4-inch loaf pan lined with aluminum foil and lightly greased. Sprinkle the crushed candy canes or peppermint candies liberally over the top. Pop the candy into the coldest part of your freezer and let sit, undisturbed, for 8–9 minutes until set. Unmold or slice into small squares and enjoy!

Store in an airtight container at room temperature, or in the fridge if your kitchen is warmer than 65°F.

6 Ounces (About 1 Cup) Bittersweet Chocolate Chips

¼ Cup Coconut Oil

¼ Teaspoon Peppermint Extract

¼ Teaspoon Salt

2 Ounces Crushed Candy Canes or Peppermint Hard Candies (About ½ Cup)

S'mores Baked Alaska

The polar ice caps are melting and global temperatures are rising at an alarming rate, but this miniature edible iceberg still manages to keep its cool in the face of a smoldering flame. Resting upon a sturdy graham cracker platform, creamy scoops of chocolate ice cream remain insulated by a frothy meringue cloak. Toasting to a marshmallowy consistency, the overall effect is that of an indoor s'more, complete with the excitement of an open fire. If only climate change had such an easy fix!

These treats can be finished either in the oven or with a kitchen torch. I find it easier to use a kitchen torch, but there's no need to run out and buy any fancy equipment if you don't already have one. Just set the broiler on your oven to its highest setting when you're ready to bring the heat.

Set out the graham cracker squares on a baking sheet and top each with scoop of ice cream, no larger than the base so that it won't hang over the edge. Place the whole baking sheet into your freezer to re-solidify the ice cream.

Pour the aquafaba into the bowl of your stand mixer with the whisk attachment installed and gradually increase the speed up to its highest setting. Once you have a steady froth going, slowly sprinkle in the sugar and cream of tartar together. Whip at full power for 5–7 minutes, until you achieve a sturdy meringue that stands up at firm peaks. Gently fold in the vanilla extract.

Apply the meringue all over and around the scoop of ice cream, making sure that it completely covers the filling and connects with the graham cracker base. Either run the baking sheet under the broiler for just 1–2 minutes, or hit the individual servings with a kitchen torch, until the meringue is golden brown all over. Serve immediately before you have a meltdown!

4 Graham Cracker Squares (2 Rectangles Split in Half)

4 Scoops Vegan Chocolate Ice Cream (About ¼–⅓ Cup Each)

¼ Cup Aquafaba

⅔ Cup Granulated Sugar

¼ Teaspoon Cream of Tartar

1 Teaspoon Vanilla Extract

Speculoos Panforte

MAKES 14–18 SERVINGS

Gingerbread has nothing on this sultry Christmastime treat. The chewy mixture of fruits and nuts has been warming the winter holidays since ancient times in Italy, where the chewy, sticky sweet originally took root. Falling somewhere between candy and pastry, some undiscerning eaters deign to call it a fruitcake, but that label does nothing to honor the unique and joyous eating experience that panforte has to offer. True to its name of "strong bread," it leads with unapologetically bold seasonings. This rendition skews more heavily in favor of cinnamon, drawn from a foundation of speculoos cookie crumbs rather than plain wheat flour for a flavorful no-bake base. The exact fruits and nuts are fully interchangeable provided you don't skimp on the spices.

Line an 8-inch round cake pan with foil and lightly grease; set aside.

Place all the fruits and nuts into your food processor and pulse to break them down but not completely blend them. You want the mixture to remain very coarse and chunky. Add in the cookie crumbs, cocoa, chia seeds, spices, salt, and sugar. Pulse once or twice to combine, again taking it easy to maintain the integrity of the goodies. Drizzle the melted butter and 1 tablespoon of nondairy milk all over the mixture, and pulse to incorporate. You should now have a sticky dough that holds together when pressed, but if it remains slightly dry, go ahead and mix in the remaining tablespoon of milk.

Transfer to your prepared pan and use lightly moistened palms to firmly press it down into one even layer. Toss it into your freezer and chill until firm, at least 6–7 minutes.

Use the foil like a sling to pull the full round out of the pan, and slice it into thin wedges. Dust with confectioner's sugar to serve, if desired.

Leftovers can be wrapped and stored in the fridge for up to a week.

½ Cup Whole Toasted Almonds

¼ Cup Whole Toasted Hazelnuts

½ Cup Golden or Standard Raisins

¼ Cup Dried Figs, Chopped

2 Cups (About 7 Ounces) Finely Ground Speculoos Cookie Crumbs

1 Tablespoon Dutch-Processed Cocoa Powder

1 Tablespoon Chia Seeds

1 Teaspoon Ground Cinnamon

½ Teaspoon Ground Ginger

¼ Teaspoon Ground Black Pepper

¼ Teaspoon Ground Cloves

¼ Teaspoon Ground Nutmeg

¼ Teaspoon Salt

¼ Cup Dark Brown Sugar, Firmly Packed

½ Cup Vegan Butter, Melted

1–2 Tablespoons Plain Nondairy Milk

Confectioner's Sugar (Optional)

Quick Tip: Can't decide on the best fruits and nuts to employ, or simply want to skip all the extra measuring? Go ahead and toss in 1½ cups of your favorite trail mix blend instead of the almonds, hazelnuts, raisins, and figs.

White Chocolate Peanut Butter Fudge

MAKES ABOUT 16 SERVINGS

White chocolate gets a bad rap from a history of ill-fated collaborations with subpar waxy fillers and flavorless sugar bombs, but the genuine article is an entirely different beast. Pure cocoa butter is irreplaceable, imparting the transcendent aroma of true white chocolate without any sketchy additives to get in the way. Melted down and blended with everyone's favorite nut butter, it magically transforms into the most decadent fudge you've ever sunk your teeth into. Rich, thick, and creamy without being achingly sweet, these voluptuous little cubes will satisfy no matter how small you slice them.

Beat the peanut butter in a large bowl to loosen it up, making it easier to mix in the confectioner's sugar and salt. Stir slowly to prevent any of the dry powder from flying out, mixing until fairly well incorporated. Pour in the melted cocoa butter along with the vanilla, stirring thoroughly until the sticky mixture is completely homogenous.

Line a loaf pan with aluminum foil and lightly grease. Pour the peanut butter mixture into the prepared pan, smoothing out the top and tapping it gently on the counter to release any air bubble. Slide it into your freezer and let rest, undisturbed, for at least 10 minutes or until firm and sliceable. Cut into small squares with a sharp knife.

Once set, the finished fudge can be stored at room temperature in an airtight container for up to a week.

1¼ Cups Crunchy Peanut Butter

1 Cup Confectioner's Sugar

½ Teaspoon Salt

½ Cup (4 Ounces) Cocoa Butter, Melted

1 Teaspoon Vanilla Extract

Quick Tip: For a spicy change of pace, try using an equal measure of speculoos spread, either creamy or crunchy, instead of peanut butter to create a sweet, cinnamon-scented treat.

Unapologetic chocoholic? I got you. Replace the cocoa butter with an equal amount of bittersweet or unsweetened chopped dark chocolate for a classic fudge treat. If using sweetened chocolate, add sugar sparingly, according to taste.

Whole Fruit Whip

MAKES 3–4 SERVINGS

A certain theme park chain best known for its plucky cartoon mouse mascot has another claim to fame, found primarily in more temperate outposts. A soft-serve concoction of artificially flavored banana and pineapple "cream," strident fans of this frozen treat speculate about exactly what makes it so addictive. Ingredients for the powdered mix can be readily found online, and yet it still holds some mysterious magic. The craziest part of the conundrum is the fact that it's effortless to whip up right at home with whole fruits and not a speck of sugar. For an authentic vacation experience right in the comfort of your kitchen, go one step further to make a float by layering the fresh blend into tall glasses and dousing with chilled pineapple soda or just straight pineapple juice.

Chop the bananas into rough chunks and place them into your food processor along with the pineapple pieces and vanilla extract. Pulse to break down the fruit, pausing to scrape down the sides of the bowl with your spatula as needed. Continue to blend while slowly streaming in the nondairy milk until smooth and creamy. Serve immediately before it melts away!

3 Frozen Medium Bananas, Sliced (About 1 Pound)

2 Cups Cubed Frozen Pineapple

½ Teaspoon Vanilla Extract

2–4 Tablespoons Plain Nondairy Milk

Quick Tip: Always keep a stash of ripe, peeled bananas in your freezer to whip up this sweet treat whenever the craving strikes. Wait until the peels are almost completely brown for the sweetest, most intense banana flavor and stash them in ziplock freezer bags. They'll keep pretty much indefinitely, but it's unlikely they'll hang around too long with this formula on hand.

Index